Growing Up in God's Word

Bible Curriculum

"... from childhood you have known the Holy Scriptures..."
(II Timothy 3:15, NKJV)

Parables of Jesus

*Cover image: "Jesus Teaches the People by the Sea" by James Tissot
Public Domain Image*

Written and illustrated by Heather M. Pryor

Table of Contents

Introduction

Why teach children the Bible using only the Bible? Can they understand it? Yes! Is it too boring? No! I have taught a children's Bible class on Sunday mornings for over twenty years and have home-schooled my three children, teaching them the Bible in our home. Guess what? Children are a lot smarter than we give them credit for! There are just a few key things to remember in teaching the Bible to children. First, we need to be enthusiastic about the Bible ourselves. If children see that we think the Bible is boring, they will most likely adopt the same opinion. Be excited about opening the word of God together! Second, don't be afraid to tell them you don't know know an answer to their question. There are many things in the Bible that we have questions about; some things we are able to study and find an answer for, others will have to wait until we get to heaven and can ask God. It's okay to let them know you're stumped too, but encourage them to search for the answer with you. Third, set the bar high for them. Please, please, please don't "dumb" the Bible down to "their level". Children can understand a lot through patient explanation and teaching. For example, if you read a hard word in the Bible that they may not be familiar with, stop and ask them what they think it means, then give them a correct definition. Now they have learned a new word and understand the passage you've just read at the same time. Children like to be challenged and to meet our expectations for them.

The method in this curriculum works because it has been tried among many children of different ages, abilities and levels. Here is the best proof I can offer to you: One of my regular Sunday morning students brought a friend to our class one day. She answered a few questions but mostly sat very quietly, absorbing everything that was going on. Later on, the woman that brought her to church said that the little girl told her on the way home that she wanted to come to our Sunday school class every week because we *"actually teach from the Bible"*. This little girl is not "unchurched" by any means; in fact, she regularly attends a denominational megachurch every Sunday. As the scripture says, "Out of the mouths of babes!"

May your children be like Timothy who, *"from childhood has known the holy Scriptures"* (II Timothy 3:15) and may God bless you as you study His word together.

How to Use this Curriculum

Life began in a garden, so we will be using garden references and symbols throughout this curriculum to designate the different activities. Luke 8:11 says that *"the seed is the word of God"*. Our hearts are the soil that the seed needs to be planted in. We should desire to cultivate the soil of our hearts and the hearts of our children to receive the word so that it will grow and produce good fruit for our Lord.

"Growing In The Word": Lesson Text & Discussion

This is the most important part of the curriculum – the teaching of God's Word. The lesson text is broken down into manageable sections to be read aloud and then discussed. If children are old enough to read, let them read out loud. If there are several verses to be read as a section, you could take turns reading a couple of verses per person. If it helps your child, let them jot down notes or write down definitions to new words as you discuss the passage. Encourage them to ask questions and ask them leading questions to get them thinking. The discussion section is basically a paraphrasing of what was just read to make sure there is comprehension of the material. Frequently there are questions to be answered during the discussion phase as well. The section of verses often leave off at a "cliffhanger" moment which helps keep the children engaged. You read and discuss and then you're ready to read on to see what happens next. At the end of this section of the curriculum there are review questions. These can be used in several ways: You may ask them at the end of the lesson, at the end of the week for a review, or if you want to have a graded assignment, you can use them as an oral or written quiz.

*A word about translations. It is important to use a reliable and accurate translation. Some dependable ones are KJV, NKJV, ESV and ASV. Many modern translations have compromised the integrity of the Scriptures in trying to put it in "easier to understand" language. **All references in this curriculum are taken from the New King James Version.**

"Putting Down Roots": Memory Work

Memory work should be practiced every day for the entire week. Use whatever method works the best according to your child's learning style. Here is a link with a list of aids for memorizing scripture: http://pryorconvictions.com/memorizing-scripture/ The Psalmist said in Psalm 119:11, *"Thy word have I hid in my heart that I might not sin against Thee."* I cannot stress enough how important it is to memorize Scripture. In addition to Scripture, sometimes there are other items included in the Memory Work such as lists of things or categories. A challenge to parents: memorize it with your children!

"Add A Leaf": Words To Know

There are no mapping exercises for this book as there are in many other books in this series. Instead, this book includes an "Add a Leaf" section which will be words to define in each lesson. Each child needs to have a folder with notebook paper for this section (or definitions may be written in this workbook). For each lesson, write the lesson number, under it write the words to know, look up the definitions, and copy them.

"Harvest Fun": Games & Activities

There are games and activities for each lesson to help review and reinforce the material that was covered. It is best to read through these at the beginning of the week to see if any planning ahead needs to be done.

"Digging Deeper": Research

This is primarily for the older students who are able to work independently. If your younger children wish to do these assignments with your help, then by all means, let them! It is a good idea to keep a notebook for these written assignments. These assignments are meant to encourage students of the Bible to learn how to study a topic deeper by using other resources to shed light on the subject. Primarily, books and the Internet will be your sources of information so it's important to do two things: 1) Check the reliability of your source, and 2) Check multiple sources; you might find two or more very different theories or opinions. Some good resources to use are Bible commentaries, concordances (such as Strong's), Bible dictionaries (such as Easton's), Bible atlases and Bible software. There are many things we run across in the Bible that we would like to know more about. Have fun exploring!

"Food For Thought": Puzzles

There are at least two puzzles with each lesson to, again, provide review and reinforcement or just to have fun! The puzzles may be worked in the book or photocopied. All puzzle answers are provided in the Answer Key in the back of the book.

"Fruits Of Our Labor": Crafts

There are at least two crafts to do with each lesson. They vary in level of difficulty, but are another means of reinforcement of material covered. Crafts are a good activity for the kinesthetic (hands-on) learner as well as a tangible reminder for the visual learner. Please read ahead early in the week to see what materials you may need to gather in advance.

Suggested Schedule

This curriculum is designed to be used five days a week, 30 minutes to 1 hour per day. It is designed to be used with multiple ages with some activities geared toward older children and others geared toward younger. You may use as many or as few of the activities listed as you choose. Please feel free to alter the suggested schedule to fit the time constraints and needs of your family. However, the lesson and memory work portions should be used for all ages.

Begin or end each day's activities with prayer.

- Day 1 – Read "Growing in the Word": Lesson Text and Discussion. Begin "Putting Down Roots": Memory Work assignments.

- Day 2 – Continue memory work, do "Add a Leaf": Words to Know, and "Harvest Fun": Games and Activities.

- Day 3 – Continue memory work, do "Digging Deeper": Research activities, and/or "Food for Thought": Puzzles.

- Day 4 – Continue memory work, do "Fruits of Our Labor": Crafts, or continue working on previous activities.

- Day 5 – Recite memory work, do lesson Review Questions and finish any assignments or activities from the week that time didn't permit.

A Word About Parables

Why did Jesus teach in parables? Parables were an effective way to convey a spiritual lesson through common life experiences that people could easily understand and/or relate to then and still do today. Just saying the words "a prodigal son" or "a good Samaritan" immediately conjures up a descriptive picture in our minds.

It is hard to determine an exact number of parables Jesus taught since some are clearly defined in the Scriptures as a parable and others are simply classified as a parable because they fit the definition even though they may be just a one or two sentence comparison. Whether it is 39, 46 or somewhere in between, every parable and comparison Jesus taught is valuable for us to study and learn from.

This study includes 20 of the parables of Jesus, and it is our prayer that each one will be beneficial to you as you grow in God's Word.

Lesson 1: Jesus Teaches in Parables

Text: Matthew 13:10-13, 31-35, 44-46

"Growing In The Word": Lesson Text & Discussion

We are beginning a study of the parables of Jesus, but did you know that parables are not just found in the New Testament? Back in the Old Testament, Nathan the prophet came to King David and told him a story about a rich man who had many lambs but stole the one and only much-loved lamb from a poor man. Nathan was telling a story about something David could easily understand (a cruel theft) but that also had a very specific meaning for him. The purpose of Nathan's parable was to teach David a lesson – a lesson that he had sinned and needed to repent because he had stolen the wife of another man. (You can read the parable in II Samuel 12:1-9.)

Parables are not just entertaining stories; they have a specific purpose. A parable is an earthly story with a spiritual meaning. It makes a comparison between things we see and experience in this life with heavenly or spiritual things. They help us to understand certain things we don't know spiritually by comparing them to things we do know in everyday life.

Jesus was and still is the greatest teacher ever, and one of the ways he taught people was through the many parables we see recorded throughout the gospels. Some of them were long stories with lots of detail, and others were very short and simple. In this first lesson, we will look at four parables of Jesus that are only one or two verses long, yet still carry a lot of meaning.

Read Matthew 13:10-11. What question did the disciples ask Jesus in verse ten? ("*Why do You speak to them in parables?*") Up to this point in Jesus' ministry, he had preached to the people, but he had not yet used the teaching tool of parables. In the beginning of Matthew 13, Jesus taught the parable of the soils (which we will study in a later lesson). It was after this parable that the disciples asked the question. Jesus answers them by talking about "*the mysteries of the kingdom of heaven.*" When we think of a mystery, we usually think about a crime or something puzzling that needs to be solved, but when we see the word "mystery" in the Bible, it is not talking about something that can't be understood but about something that is secret, hidden, or has not yet been revealed. Parables were going to serve two purposes: 1) They would reveal the mysteries of the kingdom. 2) They would conceal the mysteries of the kingdom. How can that be? How can the same parable reveal something to one person but hide it from another? Jesus is going to explain that in the next two verses.

Read Matthew 13:12-13. Anyone who listened to the parables of Jesus could hear the words he spoke, but it was up to them if they were listening with a heart of faith. Sometimes we hear, but we do not listen. For example, picture in your mind a classroom full of children and a teacher standing up in the front of the room reading a long passage from a boring textbook. Now, picture a girl sitting in a desk near the window staring at a bird perched on a branch of the tree right outside the window. She becomes absorbed in watching this bird because it is a mama feeding her three little ones in their nest. She wonders what kind of insects the mama bird is feeding the little ones and what kind of birds they are. Her mind wanders deep into the world of nature for the next several minutes. Now, was the girl able to hear the sound of her teacher's voice all of that time? (Yes) Did the girl *listen* to what was actually being said? (No) The point is, the girl was not interested in what the teacher had to say, so although she heard the words of the teacher, she wasn't really listening and trying to understand them. So it was with the people Jesus spoke parables to. Some were greatly interested in what he was trying to teach them and gave him their full attention and believed him while others didn't like him, didn't believe in him, and didn't have any interest in being taught. It was all about their hearts.

Read Matthew 13:31-32. From verse 24 through verse 53, Jesus tells seven parables. One of the shorter ones is found in these two verses. Jesus compares the kingdom of heaven to a mustard seed. Do you like mustard? Maybe you like to put lots of runny yellow mustard on your hot dogs or hamburgers. Did you know that mustard is made by grinding mustard seeds and mixing the ground mustard powder with water, vinegar and other seasonings? Mustard seeds are so tiny that it can take as many as 1,000 of them to make an 8 oz. bottle of mustard! In Bible times, there were some kinds of mustard that had extremely tiny seeds, and yet, they grew to be a tall shrub or tree around ten to twelve feet high. In this parable, Jesus compares the kingdom of heaven to a tiny mustard seed. First of all, what is the kingdom of heaven? Think about a kingdom, maybe one you've learned about in school or seen in a movie. The kingdom has a king who rules over his subjects. If the subjects love their king, they obey him and live in his kingdom, where he rules and reigns. Christ Jesus is King, and he is the head of his church which is the kingdom. All those who love him and obey him will belong to his kingdom, the church, because they have submitted themselves (become subjects) to the rule and reign of Christ in their hearts. The mustard seed shows us several things about the kingdom of heaven: 1) The church grew great and spread throughout the world even though it came from a tiny beginning. When the church of Jesus Christ began in Acts 2, it started in one city, Jerusalem. Now, you can find the Lord's church all over the world! 2) The church grew because life was in the seed. The seed is the Word of God (Luke 8:11) and when it is planted (preached and taught), it will grow. A cool thing to try is to carefully cut open a large seed like a kidney bean. Do you know what you will find inside? A tiny plant ready to grow. Life is in a seed. 3) The church grew because the seed was planted.

That kidney bean seed will never grow if it is not planted in the soil and watered and given light. The church grows when seed (the Word of God) is planted in the hearts of people. In the parable, a man planted the mustard seed in his field in order for it to grow. 4) The church is a welcome refuge for those willing to come to it. When the mustard seed grew into a tree, what benefit was it to the birds? (They came and nested in its branches.) Jesus taught the people a lot about the kingdom of heaven from the example of one tiny little mustard seed!

Read Matthew 13:33. Now, Jesus compares the kingdom of heaven to leaven. What is leaven? Leaven is any kind of substance that is added to dough to make it rise. Usually it is yeast, but it can also be something like baking powder. I like to make homemade pizza (I've even shared my recipe with you in the Activities section!), and when I do, I add yeast to the dough. I only use a little bit, about one spoonful, to make a whole pizza. Once the yeast is dissolved in water and mixed in the dough, you can't see it anymore, but you can definitely see what it does! If I spread the dough out in my pizza pan and leave it in a warm place for awhile, the dough will rise. Why? Because of the influence of the yeast, the leaven. In this parable, who hid leaven in the dough? (A woman) Notice that the leaven doesn't get in the dough by accident or by magic; someone has to put it there. Can the church grow if no one is "hiding the leaven"? (No!) How much of the meal (dough) was affected by the leaven? (All of it) The leaven itself can't be seen, it works slowly and quietly, but it affects all of the dough, and we see what it does. If we hear the Word of God preached and allow it to work in our life, it will influence everything we do, not just part of what we do, and others should see that influence in our lives. The kingdom of heaven should act like leaven and have an influence not only in our lives but in the world.

Read Matthew 13:34-35. According to verse 35, why did Jesus speak to the people in parables? (It fulfilled a prophecy.) When Jesus spoke in parables, it fulfilled a prophecy that was made in the Old Testament which is quoted in this verse. Do you know which Old Testament verse is quoted? (Psalm 78:2)

Read Matthew 13:44. In Bible times, if you had a large amount of money or some valuable possessions like jewelry or something made of gold, etc., it was hard to find a place to keep them safe. You couldn't just go to the store and buy a safe to put them in. So, many people would bury their valuables on their land. Sometimes a landowner would die without revealing where his valuables were hidden, or he might have forgotten where he buried them. I once buried a yogurt cup with a quarter inside it in my backyard. I did this because my kids were studying about archaeology in our home school so we practiced making a grid for a dig in the backyard where I had previously buried several items. We never did find the quarter and probably never will. Years from now, someone may be digging in my backyard, and they are going to find some buried treasure! In this parable, a man accidentally finds some buried treasure. Where was it? (In a field) Can you imagine how exciting that was for him? He immediately hides it again. Why do you think he did that? (To keep it safe) What did he do next? (He sold all that he had so he could buy the field.) He knew how valuable the treasure was so he did all he could to buy that field which would also mean he would own whatever was in it. It was so important to him to possess that treasure for his own that he was willing to give up everything else he owned in order to have it. So, how is the kingdom of heaven like hidden treasure? Is it valuable? Is it worth looking for? Is it important enough to sacrifice everything else in our lives? Yes!

Read Matthew 13:45-46. This parable may seem very similar to the one about hidden treasure – they both talk about something valuable that was found by someone willing to sacrifice everything for it. But there are some differences. First of all, what does Jesus compare the kingdom of heaven to in this parable? (A merchant seeking beautiful pearls) The kingdom is not compared to the valuable pearl but to the man who was looking for the pearl. Second, the man who found the hidden treasure found it by accident, but the man who found the pearl of great price was deliberately looking for such a treasure. As a pearl merchant, he was always searching for good, quality pearls. He would immediately recognize one that was of great value because he knew so much about pearls. What was he willing to do when he found such a valuable pearl? (He was willing to sell everything that he had in order to buy it.) Have you ever played "Hide and Seek?" To seek is to look carefully for something. What does **Matthew 6:33** tell us to seek? (The Kingdom of God) There are many people in the world who are searching – searching for something that matters, searching for something of real value, searching for truth. The kingdom of heaven is a true treasure to those seekers.

Review Questions: (Answers are provided in the Answer Key.)

1. What is the purpose of a parable?
2. What is an example of a parable found in the Old Testament?
3. What parable did Jesus teach in the beginning of Matthew 13?
4. When we see the word "mystery" in the Bible, what does it mean?
5. Why did some people understand the parables of Jesus while others did not?
6. In what city did the church of Jesus Christ begin?
7. Where in the Bible do we read about the beginning of the church?
8. What is inside a seed?

9. How does the church grow?

10. How is the kingdom of heaven like leaven?

11. What verse in the Old Testament prophesied that Jesus would open his mouth in parables?

12. How is the kingdom of heaven like hidden treasure?

13. In the parable of the pearl of great price, what is the kingdom of heaven compared to?

14. What are two differences in the parables of the hidden treasure and the pearl of great price?

15. What does Matthew 6:33 tell us to seek?

 ## "Putting Down Roots": Memory Work

- Memorize Psalm 78:1-2

- Memorize Matthew 13:44

 ## "Add A Leaf": Words To Know

- Parable

- Leaven

 ## "Harvest Fun": Games & Activities

- Locate the Leaven – Leaven was very significant to the Jews, especially during the Passover feast. As the Passover was celebrated down through the years by the

Jews, the evening before the Passover feast began, the head of the family would lead his family through the house by candlelight, searching for leaven. No leaven of any kind was allowed to be in the house during the length of the Passover feast which was 7 days. Sometimes Jewish families would sell their leaven to their Gentile neighbors for the length of Passover, then buy it back when Passover was over. Leaven is any kind of agent, like yeast or baking powder, that causes bread to rise. The woman in the parable from this lesson used leaven in her baking – she "hid" it in three measures of meal. Hide a package of yeast in the house or write the word "leaven" on a small index card and hide it. Then search the house to locate the leaven. Take turns hiding it, or hide several and see who can find the most.

- Homemade Pizza Dough – In the parable of leaven, the woman hid leaven in some meal. She was baking something and the leaven was going to make her dough rise. You're going to "hide" the leavening agent of yeast in pizza dough and watch the effect it will have. Here are the ingredients you will need to gather to make the dough:

   - 1 pkg. of rapid rise yeast

   - 1 cup of warm water

   - 1 tsp. each of salt and sugar

   - 2 T. olive oil

   - 2 ½ to 3 cups all-purpose flour

First, sprinkle the package of yeast over the warm water and gently stir. Set it aside for a few minutes. Add in the salt and sugar and stir until dissolved. Add in the olive oil and stir. Begin adding flour, about 2 cups at first and stir until well-mixed. Keep adding flour until the dough forms a ball when stirred and starts cleaning the side of the bowl. Lightly flour a surface to knead the dough and begin the kneading process. To knead dough, pull the top of the half of the dough over on the bottom half, pressing down with the base of the palms of your hands. Then turn the dough a quarter turn counterclockwise and repeat. (It sounds more complicated than it is. It's actually fun to play with dough!) You only need to knead for a couple of minutes until the ball of dough is nice and smooth and elastic. Lightly spray a pizza pan with cooking spray, place the ball of dough in the middle then gently start pressing it out to fill the pan. *Tip: Butter the tips of your fingers to keep the dough from sticking to them. Place the pan in a warm area or on top of your oven while it is preheating. After about 20-30 minutes, check your pizza pan. Did your dough rise? If your yeast was fresh and did its leavening work, it should have. Now you can top your dough with your favorite sauce and toppings. Bake at 450 degrees for about 18-20 minutes. When you eat your pizza, you won't see or taste the leaven (yeast), but your dough wouldn't have risen nicely without. Its influence is clearly seen.

 "Digging Deeper": Research

- Mustard seeds and trees – Find some images of mustard seeds and trees. Notice how tiny the seed is as compared to how large a shrub or tree it grows into. What are some different species of mustard? What kind of seeds does each species produce and what are the differences in their flavors? How large can a mustard tree grow to be and how long does it take to reach maturity (the point that it can be harvested)?

- Pearls – It is fascinating to learn how pearls are formed naturally! Research this process and try to answer the following questions: Where do pearls "grow?" How long does it take to form a pearl? What is the record for the largest natural pearl ever discovered? Learning about this process may help you see why the pearl merchant in the parable was willing to give up so much to possess something so valuable.

"Food For Thought": Puzzles

- Which Parable? - We studied four short parables of Jesus in this lesson. Read the following clues, then choose the correct answer from the box, and write it on the line. Answers will be used more than once, and some clues have more than one answer. Answers are provided in the Answer Key.

Parable of the mustard seed	Parable of the leaven
Parable of the hidden treasure	Parable of the pearl of great price

1. Which parable mentions a woman? _____

2. Which parable mentions someone buying something? _____

   _____

3. In which parable does something go from small to large? _____

   _____

4. Which parable compares something to the kingdom of heaven? _____

   _____

5. Which parable mentions someone rejoicing? _____

6. Which parable mentions a field? _____

7. Which parable mentions something that is hidden? _____

   _____

8. Which parable mentions an object that surpassed all others? _____

   _____

9. Which parable mentions having to sell something before buying something else?

    _____

10. Which parable has something that benefits birds? _____

- Word Search Puzzle - There were a couple of hidden items in the parables you studied. See if you can find all of the hidden words from this lesson. Answers are provided in the Answer Key.

```
N A M O W D D L O S G H L O R
N R U J E N W J U N T A E L H
H A S Y E P C S I E H L T A I
B F T V O F E H C V B R H V D
C I A R U J C A N A E E G U D
M E R C H A N T R E A S U R E
H L D D E L B A U L A V O A N
T D E T S W P D G E O O B A A
```

parable	treasure	teaching
heaven	field	Jesus
leaven	hidden	joy
woman	mustard	bought
pearl	tree	sold
merchant	birds	valuable

"Fruits Of Our Labor": Crafts

- Pearl in an Oyster – There are two options for this craft, one edible and one not. To make a simple "pearl in an oyster" craft, use small white paper plates (dessert size) and completely color one side pink. Fold the plate in half, pink side in, then glue a cotton ball in the middle of the creased pink side. To make an edible craft, bake plain sugar cookies or purchase Nilla wafers. Tint vanilla frosting light pink and spread on the bottom of one cookie. Position a second cookie on top, slightly tilted up to mimic an open shell. Position a small white gumball or white ball candy (like Sixlets found online or at party supply stores) in the frosting to represent the pearl.

- Treasure Box – One of the hidden items in the parables was treasure. Everyone has things that are special and valuable to them, and it is nice to have a pretty box to keep those treasures in. Purchase a plain wooden box from a craft store, then paint it and decorate it any way you would like.

- Illustrate a parable - Throughout this book, one of the craft ideas for each lesson will be to illustrate a parable from the lesson. This can be done by drawing, painting, chalk, or in rebus fashion (*See rebus explanation.) There will be instructions in the last lesson as to how to assemble all of your illustrated parables into a book. For this lesson, choose one parable to illustrate or illustrate all of them if you'd like.

*Rebus explanation – A rebus puzzle is a combination of pictures, letters, numbers and symbols which stand for words. For example, if you were illustrating the words "Be nice" in a rebus fashion, you could draw a picture of a bee - "e" for the word "be". Then you could write the letter "n", add a + sign, then draw a picture of an ice cube. (n + ice = nice). Get it?

Lesson 2: Parable of the Good Samaritan

Text: Luke 10:25-37

"Growing In The Word": Lesson Text & Discussion

Read Luke 10:25. A lawyer was asking Jesus a question. Lawyers were sometimes called scribes and they were basically professional teachers of the Law of Moses. Many of these lawyers and scribes and Pharisees would purposely try to trick Jesus or see if they could ask him a question he couldn't or wouldn't answer according to the law. This lawyer was trying to do just that. What question did he ask Jesus? ("What shall I do to inherit eternal life?")

Read Luke 10:26-27. Jesus turns the tables on him by asking him to answer his own question by stating what the scripture says. What did the lawyer answer with? (Scriptures from the Old Testament: "You shall love the Lord your God with all your heart, with all your soul, with all your strength, and with all your mind and your neighbor as yourself.") The lawyer, who was knowledgeable in the law, quoted from two verses in the Old Testament. The first one was Deuteronomy 6:5 about loving God and the second was Leviticus 19:18 about loving your neighbor.

Read Luke 10:28-29. Did Jesus say the lawyer had answered his own question correctly? (Yes) But the lawyer didn't stop there. Continuing to try to put Jesus to the test and wanting to make himself look good as a righteous man, he then asked another question. What was it? ("Who is my neighbor?") Since he had just quoted the verse about loving your neighbor, now the lawyer wanted Jesus to tell him exactly who his neighbor is. Jesus will answer this question with a parable.

Read Luke 10:30. The road from Jerusalem to Jericho was a well-used public road. The problem was bands of robbers who would hide along the route and take advantage of single travelers, such as this man, or very small groups of travelers that they could outnumber. This is why many people traveled in large groups or caravans; it would be safer. What did the thieves do to the traveler? (Stripped him, wounded him, and left him half dead)

Read Luke 10:31-32. Two different men approach at different times and see this poor man lying there wounded. Who were the two men? (A priest and a Levite) It would be quite common for them to be traveling on this road. They would have religious duties at the temple in Jerusalem and Jericho served as a home base for many of them. Both of these men are what you would call "church" people. They were religious and the priest in particular was a religious leader of the Jews. What did they both do? (They passed by on the other side of the road.) Not only did they not want to help this man, but they wanted to keep as far away from him as possible! The law of Moses commanded mercy and help to others, yet these two ignore the law and the poor wounded man. How sad that they saw someone who clearly needed help, yet they did nothing. This should remind us how important it is to be on the lookout for opportunities to help others and then be willing to do what we can as the Lord has commanded us.

Read Luke 10:33. As a Samaritan approaches and sees the wounded man, what does he feel? (Compassion) What does "compassion" mean? It is pity, sympathy, or suffering with another. The wounded man is most likely a Jew and the Jews and Samaritans couldn't stand each other. John 4:9 says, "*Jews have no dealings with Samaritans.*" The Jews even made it a point not to travel through the land of Samaria unless they absolutely had to, just to avoid the people. Now, here's a Samaritan man who sees this Jewish man and feels pity and kindness toward him.

Read Luke 10:34-35. The Samaritan does not pass by on the other side as the priest and Levite have done. He stops and helps the man. What does he do for him first? (He pours oil and wine on his wounds and bandages them.) The oil and wine would have been used for medicinal purposes. They were often mixed together and would have cleaned the wounds making them sanitary and then aided in healing. The Samaritan then bandaged the wounds. When we have an open cut, we clean it, put something like Neosporin on it, and then bandage it. After giving first aid, what does the Samaritan do next? (He puts the wounded man on his own animal, takes him to an inn, and takes care of him.) We don't know where the Samaritan was heading or if he had a schedule to keep, but it didn't matter. He took the time to care for the poor, wounded man the rest of that day and night. What does the Samaritan do the next morning? (He gives the innkeeper money to take care of the wounded man.) As he went on his way the next morning, he didn't just leave the man on his own with no resources. Remember, the man had been robbed and probably had no money. The Samaritan made sure he left enough money to provide for the man's needs and even offered to pay more if it was needed when he came back later.

Read Luke 10:36. After finishing the parable, Jesus asks the lawyer a question in order to answer his own question. Remember the lawyer had asked Jesus, "Who is my neighbor?" What does Jesus now ask him? ("Which of these three do you think was neighbor to him who fell among the thieves?")

Read Luke 10:37. How does the lawyer answer Jesus? (The one who showed mercy) The lawyer, being a Jew, has to admit the truth from this story. The priest and Levite, who were Jews, did not show any compassion or mercy to the wounded man, but completely ignored him and left him for dead. The Samaritan obviously showed mercy, and therefore was a kind neighbor to the wounded man. What does Jesus then tell the lawyer to do? (The same)

He wants this lawyer to see that anyone who needs help is his neighbor, not just the people he likes or wants to help. This is an excellent lesson for us to learn as well. We are not to show kindness only to our friends or people we know or like, but to everyone, including people who we might even think are our enemies. We are to be merciful as our Lord is merciful.

Review Questions: (Answers are provided in the Answer Key.)

1. Who stood up and asked Jesus a question?
2. Why did he do this?
3. What question did he ask Jesus first?
4. How did Jesus respond?
5. What two scriptures did the lawyer quote?
6. Did Jesus say the lawyer had answered right or wrong?
7. What was the next question the lawyer asked Jesus?
8. In the parable, where was the traveler going?
9. What did the thieves do to the traveler?
10. Who passed by first?
11. Who passed by second?
12. Who passed by third?
13. Who had compassion on the wounded man?
14. What did he do for the traveler?
15. Whom did he pay to continue the man's care?
16. What did Jesus ask the lawyer at the conclusion of the parable?
17. What answer did the lawyer give?
18. What did Jesus tell him to do?

"Putting Down Roots": Memory Work

- Memorize Deuteronomy 6:5

- Memorize Leviticus 19:18

- Memorize Mark 12:30-31

"Add A Leaf": Words To Know

- Compassion

- Denarius

"Harvest Fun": Games & Activities

- Test the Teacher – Jesus, the Teacher, was being tested by a lawyer in our lesson. Test your teacher by asking him or her some questions from the lesson. You could use the review questions from this lesson or make up some of your own. (Don't be too hard on them!) You could even test their knowledge of the memory verses or words to know.

- Be a Good Samaritan – Have one person play the part of the "injured" person. Each player will have one minute when it is their turn to figure out how to be a good Samaritan and help the person in the way that he needs. You may use props if you'd like. To start, the injured person will say what the injury is. For example, "I fell and scraped my arm up pretty bad", or "I was crossing the street with a bag of groceries and tripped and spilled them all over the ground." Some other "injuries" might include a broken ankle, a bump on the head, hurt feelings, dog broke free from the leash, a black eye, in bed with a cold, got too hot and dehydrated, received some bad news and am really sad, etc. In the one minute given, the player may race around the house to collect items needed for that "injury" and administer them. Discuss how we need to be alert to people in need all around us and be willing to show kindness and compassion as the good Samaritan did.

 ## "Digging Deeper": Research

- The Samaritans – Who were the Samaritans? Where did they come from? Why did the Jews despise them so much? How was their worship similar or different than the worship of the Jews?

- Levites – What was a Levite? What was the difference between a Levite and a priest? What were some specific duties of Levites?

- Denarii – What are denarii? What were they worth in Jesus' day?

 ## "Food For Thought": Puzzles

- Charades: Guess the character – Write the following characters on slips of paper. Take turns drawing a slip and acting it out so that everyone can guess the character from the lesson. (Lawyer, Jesus, Levite, traveler, priest, robber, innkeeper, Samaritan)

- Sequence – Put the events of the lesson in the proper order, numbering them from 1-10. Answers are provided in the Answer Key.

  _____ A priest came down that road and passed by on the other side.

  _____ The lawyer, wanting to justify himself, asked Jesus, "Who is my neighbor?"

  _____ He took out two denarii and gave them to the innkeeper.

  _____ A man went down to Jericho and fell among thieves who left him half dead.

  _____ "Which of these three do you think was neighbor to him who fell among the thieves?"

  _____ A certain lawyer stood up and tested Jesus.

  _____ A Levite arrived at the place and looked, then passed by on the other side.

  _____ He went to him, bandaged his wounds, pouring on oil and wine.

  _____ Jesus said, "Go and do likewise."

  _____ A certain Samaritan saw him and had compassion on him.

 "Fruits Of Our Labor": Crafts

- Homemade Card - Make a nice homemade card with a pretty picture or stickers on the front and a Bible verse written inside. Tuck it in the front of the compassion basket. If you want to be really creative, you could rubber stamp or stencil the front of the card. If you have special scissors that cut fancy borders, you could use those too.

- Compassion Basket – The good Samaritan showed compassion to the wounded man by trying to provide items for his comfort and healing. Put together some items of comfort and healing in a basket and give it to someone who is sick or recovering from a hospital visit or surgery. You can find a variety of nice baskets at thrift stores for a good price. Line the basket with some colored tissue paper and tie a colorful bow on the handle. Fill it with items such as: soup (canned, or better yet, homemade!), Kleenex, cough drops, hand lotion, puzzle books, tea bags, candy, small bottles of Gatorade, crackers, or anything you can think of that the person would like or be able to use. Don't forget to put in your homemade card!

- Illustrate a parable - Illustrate the parable from this lesson. You can continue the same method you started with or choose a different way to illustrate it.

Lesson 3: Parables of the Lost Coin, Lost Sheep & Lost Son

Text: Luke 15:1-32

"Growing In The Word": Lesson Text & Discussion

Read Luke 15:1-3. Who wanted to hear Jesus? (Tax collectors and sinners) Jesus always seeks to save those who are lost. He was known to talk with, eat with, and teach those who the "righteous people" looked down on. The Pharisees and scribes were some of those "righteous people" who didn't think Jesus should be associating with no-good sinners! They murmured and complained among themselves about this very thing. Jesus knew what they were thinking and saying to each other so he told them three parables, all having to do with something that was lost and then was found.

Read Luke 15:4-7. Jesus tells the story of a man who has one hundred sheep, and yet one gets lost. Does he say, "It's no big deal! I have ninety-nine other ones."? (No!) He looks for that one lost sheep until he finds it. When he does find it, he's so happy and so gentle with it. Where does he carry the lost sheep? (On his shoulders) He doesn't yell at the sheep for getting lost and causing him a lot of trouble, but rather he rejoices all the way home. Not only that, when he arrives home, he calls his friends and neighbors over to rejoice with him. What does he say to them? ("Rejoice with me, for I have found my sheep which was lost!") Jesus compares this lost sheep being found to one sinner who repents. Jesus' point is that there is great joy in heaven when even one person who was lost is found through their repentance and salvation. He's trying to make the Pharisees and scribes see why he teaches and talks to sinners. They're lost! Why do the ninety-nine need no repentance? (These would be people who are saved and faithful. They are not lost so they do not need to repent.)

Read Luke 15:8-10. Jesus then told them a story of a woman who had ten silver coins and lost one. Have you ever lost any money? How hard did you look to find it? The Bible says this woman searched diligently. The coin was valuable, and she was determined to find it. She lit a lamp and swept the house with a broom to make sure she covered every possible spot. When she found the lost coin, whom did she call? (Her friends and neighbors) What did she want them to do with her? (Rejoice!) Again, there was great happiness displayed over finding the lost item. Jesus said there was great joy in the presence of whom over one sinner who repents? (The angels of God) Jesus was again emphasizing how important just one lost person is to God and the heavenly beings.

Read Luke 15:11-13. The last parable Jesus tells them is a long one about a lost son. A father had two sons and the younger one wanted his inheritance early. He wanted to spend the money now! Where did the younger son go with his money? (To a far country) What did he do with his wealth? (Wasted it!)

Read Luke 15:14-16. It didn't take long for the money to be spent completely and then to make things worse, a famine came. What is a famine? (A severe food shortage) This son now had no money, and there's a food shortage in the land so naturally, he began to get very hungry. To try to earn some money, what job did he get? (He fed pigs.) This part of the story would have really affected Jesus' listeners. The Jews never ate pork because pigs were an unclean animal according to the law of Moses. Not only did they not eat pigs, they wouldn't even touch them. So to hear that this young man had resorted to a job where he had to feed pigs would have made them think that he couldn't have sunk any lower in life. The young man in the story was so hungry, what would he have gladly filled his stomach with? (The pigs' food!) Can you imagine being so hungry that you would want to eat the food in a pig's trough? Did anyone help this young man out and give him anything? (No)

Read Luke 15:17-19. This young man finally realized how wrong he'd been. He had no one to blame for his miserable life other than himself. He decided to go back home to his father, but not as a son. What did he say he'd ask his father to make him? (A hired servant) He realized he didn't deserve to go home and have the privileges of a son again. He wanted to work for his food and place to sleep. The most important thing he admitted to himself is that he had sinned. What this young man did was repent. What does it mean to repent? Repentance is being sorry for sin, but then changing your life. It's not enough to be sorry for something you've done wrong if you don't change your behavior. It would be like a thief who gets caught stealing and says how sorry he is, only to go out the next day and steal again. He didn't repent because his being sorry didn't lead to a change in his life. The young man in the parable is not only sorry for what he's done, but he's willing to change his life and be humble.

Read Luke 15:20. Who saw the son returning when he was still a great way off from the house? (His father) Did his father run to him yelling at him for being so foolish as to blow all of his money? (No) What did the father do when he ran to his son? (He "fell on his neck" which means embraced or hugged him, and kissed him.) The father was so very glad to see his lost son returned home again. The Bible says he had compassion on him. We just talked about compassion in our last lesson of the good Samaritan. It is having pity and kindness toward someone who needs help.

Read Luke 15:21. Did the son admit his sin to his father? (Yes)

Read Luke 15:22-24. Did the father agree to his son now being a hired servant in his household? (No!) The father forgave his son and wanted to rejoice and celebrate his homecoming. What three things does he ask the servants to bring and put on his son? (The best robe, a ring for his hand and sandals for his feet) What does the father then tell the servants to do? (Kill the fatted calf) They're going to have a great feast to celebrate!

Read Luke 15:25-27. Don't forget about the other son! He'd been out in the field and came home to hear a party going on. Did he go inside to see what was going on? (No) He asked one of the servants what was happening. The servant told him the good news about his brother returning home at long last and how happy their father was. If your brother had been gone a long time or was missing and you didn't know if he was okay, would you be happy to see him safely back home?

Read Luke 15:28. Well, this brother was NOT happy! He was angry about all of this and refused to go in to the party. His father came outside to see what was wrong.

Read Luke 15:29-30. What did this son complain of? He felt that it wasn't fair that he had been a good son all of these years and had never disobeyed his father or been foolish and wasteful like his brother, and yet their father had never given him a party! He was actually jealous of the kindness and generosity that his brother was receiving. He felt that his brother didn't deserve any of it.

Read Luke 15:31-32. The father doesn't feel the same way, does he? He pointed out to his older son that everything the father owned was his too, and he was glad to have him safely with him all of his life. However, the father points out that it was right to celebrate the younger son's homecoming because he was lost and now was found. Jesus wanted the Pharisees and scribes to not only see the joy in the repentance and return of the son in this story, but he wanted them to see that they should not be like the older brother either. We should always be happy when a person who is lost spiritually truly repents and is saved. It is a cause for rejoicing!

Review Questions: (Answers are provided in the Answer Key.)

1. Who was Jesus eating with that wanted to hear him teach?

2. Who was murmuring about this?

3. In the first parable, what was lost?

4. How many others were there who were in the wilderness?

5. How did the man carry the lost one home?

6. When he arrived home, he called his friends and neighbors in to do what with him?

7. Jesus said there is more joy in heaven over one sinner who does what?

8. What did the woman lose in the second parable?

9. How many other ones did she have?

10. Where did she lose it?

11. What did she do when she found it?

12. Who was lost in the third parable?

13. What did he ask his father for?

14. What did he do with it?

15. What occurred in the land where he was living?

16. What job did he do?

17. How hungry was he?

18. What is repentance?

19. What did he want to return home as?

20. What did his father have the servants put on his son when he returned home?

21. What was killed for a feast of celebration?

22. What was the older son's reaction?

23. Who did Jesus come to seek and save?

"Putting Down Roots": Memory Work

- Memorize Luke 15:7

- Memorize Luke 15:10

"Add A Leaf": Words To Know

- Repentance
- Prodigal

"Harvest Fun": Games & Activities

- Find the lost coin – Choose one person to hide a silver half-dollar or quarter somewhere in the house. Let the other players "search diligently" to find it. The one who hid it may give "hot" or "cold" clues to help locate it. Everyone rejoice when it's found!

- Lost sheep, coin, or son – Each player needs three index cards. On one write "sheep", on another write "coin", and on the third write "son". As each clue is read, players hold up the card with the correct answer. Be careful, some clues might be tricky! Keep score if you'd like as to who answered the most correctly.

1. I got lost in the wilderness. (sheep)

2. I was in a pig pen. (son)

3. I went to a far country. (son)

4. I was one of ten. (coin)

5. I was one of one hundred. (sheep)

6. I was carried when I was found. (sheep)

7. I was kissed when I was found. (son)

8. I was rejoiced over when I was found. (sheep and coin or all)

9. My father was looking for me. (son)

10. A woman was looking for me. (coin)

11. Friends and neighbors were called together when I was found. (sheep and coin or all)

12. I was lost in a house. (coin)

13. A great feast was given when I was found. (son)

14. A lamp was lit to look for me. (coin)

15. I belonged to a man. (sheep and son)

 ## "Digging Deeper": Research

- Repentance – These three parables all dealt with a lost item and how God feels about the lost who repent. The Bible has a lot to say about repentance. See how many verses you can find that deal with repentance. Who were some preachers of repentance? Who were some examples of people who repented?

- Pharisees and scribes – Who were these two groups of people? What were their religious duties? Who was a well-known scribe? How did the group known as the Pharisees begin? What was Jesus' view of these two religious groups?

"Food For Thought": Puzzles

- Coded Message – Use the key to break the code. The answer is provided in the Answer Key.

—— —— —— —— —— —— —— —— —— ——   —— ——
9 22 11 22 13 7 26 13 24 22   18 8

—— —— —— —— ——   —— —— —— —— ——   —— —— ——
25 22 18 13 20   8 12 9 9 2   21 12 9

—— —— ——   —— —— ——   —— —— —— —— —— —— ——
8 18 13   26 13 23   7 6 9 13 18 13 20

—— ——   —— —— ——.
7 12   20 12 23

Key to the Code:

F	N	R	U	A	G	O	S	V	C	H	T	D	I	E	B	W	K	Y	P	M	L	J
21	13	9	6	26	20	12	8	5	24	19	7	23	18	22	25	4	16	2	11	14	15	17

- Crossword Puzzle – The following page contains a crossword puzzle for this lesson. If an answer has more than one word, space(s) are included. Answers are provided in the Answer Key.

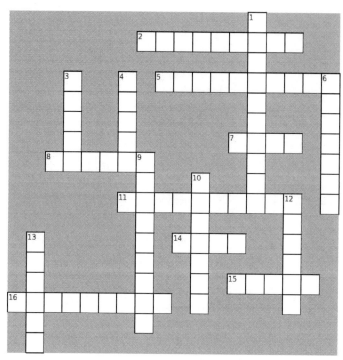

Across

2 They murmured against Jesus
5 How the woman searched for her lost coin
7 What was killed for a feast held in honor of the returned son
8 Where there is joy over one who repents
11 Where the 99 sheep were
14 A man had _____ sons
15 A man had one hundred of these and lost one
16 What the lost sheep was carried on

Down

1 A change of heart which leads to a changed life
3 Where the coin was lost
4 The kind of animals that the lost son was feeding
6 This son wanted his inheritance early
9 Who was called by the woman when she found her lost coin
10 What was done when the lost items were found
12 A woman had ten _____ coins
13 He ran to meet the lost son

"Fruits Of Our Labor": Crafts

- Lost Coin flap picture – Remember in the parable, the woman lost a coin of great value in her house. She searched with a light, she swept the whole house and didn't give up until she found her coin. Use the templates in Appendix B to make a picture with lift-able flaps. Copy both pages with the house picture. If possible, copy the first house template onto card stock. Cut out each house shape. Color the pictures if you'd like. Glue the second house template on a piece of construction paper or card stock. Take the first house template and have an adult help you use an exacto knife to cut the flaps. There are 8 flaps. Cut only on the bold black lines, not the dotted lines. The dotted lines are the fold lines. Once the flaps are cut, carefully glue the first house template over the second house template, matching them up perfectly. Use a glue stick and only place glue in spots that are not near the flaps. Once your picture is finished, you should be able to lift the flaps to see what items are in the house – and to find the lost coin! You may want to show your picture to someone else, tell them about the parable, then see if they can locate the coin. The location of the lost coin is in the Answer Key.

- Cupcake decorating – Bake and decorate cupcakes to represent the lost items in these parables. To decorate a cupcake like a sheep, frost the cupcake white, then place marshmallows on the top for its wool. Use two raisins for ears and a chocolate cookie (or part of one) for the face. Pipe dots of frosting for eyes. For coin cupcakes, frost with white or chocolate frosting then place a foil-covered chocolate coin on the top or use frosting to draw a coin. For the lost son, frost the cupcake with frosting then place a nilla wafer cookie on top for the face of the son. Pipe eyes, nose, mouth, and hair on the wafer using a round tip. Or put frosting in a baggie and snip a tiny hole in the corner to pipe frosting onto the wafer. If you bake two dozen cupcakes as most cake mixes will make, you may want to be creative and decorate the rest of the cupcakes with other items from the parables such as a ring, pig, sandal, shepherd's crook, etc. Serve these decorated cupcakes to your friends or family and explain the three parables to them.

- Illustrate a parable - Illustrate a parable from this lesson or all three if you'd like. You can continue the same method you have been using or choose a different way to illustrate it.

Lesson 4: Parable of the Unforgiving Servant

Text: Matthew 18:21-35

"Growing In The Word": Lesson Text & Discussion

Read Matthew 18:21-22. Peter had a couple of questions for Jesus about forgiveness. It's on his mind because Jesus had just finished talking about what you should do when someone sins against you. (Matthew 18:15-20) Let's talk about what forgiveness means. The word "forgiveness" in the Bible comes from a Greek word, aphesis (af'-es-is) which means "to release" or "to let go." When we forgive someone, we are to let go of the wrong they did to us and not keep bringing it up. We are to let go of any anger or hard feelings against them and treat them as the Lord would want us to. What is the first question Peter asked Jesus? ("Lord, how often shall my brother sin against me, and I forgive him?") Do you ever find it hard to forgive someone? Maybe they have treated you very unkindly or hurt you in some way and maybe it happens more than once. This is what Peter was struggling with. He's asking how many times can someone keep treating him wrong before it reaches a point that he doesn't have to forgive them anymore. Which leads to his next question... *"Up to seven times?"* No doubt Peter thought that he was being pretty generous. He was letting Jesus know that he was actually willing to forgive someone up to seven times if they sinned against him, but after that...! How did Jesus answer him? (*"I do not say to you, up to seven times, but up to seventy times seven."*) Okay, let's throw a little math in with our Bible lesson. How much is 70 x 7? (490) Do you think Jesus was telling Peter that he had to up his forgiveness limit to 490 times, or did he mean something else? Jesus was teaching Peter (and us) that forgiveness is unlimited. To illustrate the importance of forgiveness, Jesus tells him the parable of the unforgiving servant.

Read Matthew 18:23-24. The parable begins with a scene of a number of servants being brought before their king to "settle their accounts." This means the servants were paying money to the king that belonged to him, such as taxes or a debt. One servant was brought before him that owed a rather large amount. How much did this servant owe the king? (Ten thousand talents) A talent was a very valuable sum of money measured in weight of silver or gold. A talent of gold was obviously worth more than a talent of silver, but both of them were worth a lot. A debt of ten thousand talents would probably be equal to millions of dollars in our money. The point is, this man owed the king more than he could ever repay him.

Read Matthew 18:25. In ancient times, if a person had debts which he could not afford to pay, he was sometimes sold into slavery along with his family to help raise money to pay at least part of the debt. (You will learn more about this practice in one of the research projects of this lesson.) Stop and think about this for a minute. Imagine your family lived long ago during the days that Jesus walked the earth. Your father bought a large piece of land for your family to build a house on and to raise animals. He bought it from another man who agreed to let your father pay for it in full one year later. A year goes by and now your father has to pay the full amount for the land, but he doesn't have any money to pay the man. Now imagine that man telling your father that your entire family will be sold as slaves to pay the debt. How would you feel? Would you be afraid? Would you wonder what would happen to you? Would your family be able to stay together or be sold separately? What if you were sold to a cruel master? This was a terrible option that no one wanted to be faced with, but it was one that was practiced frequently long ago. The king ordered this very thing to happen to the servant and his family. What else was to be sold? (Everything the servant owned) How do you think the servant will react to this command of the king?

Read Matthew 18:26. The servant doesn't get mad and argue with the king or act like this is no big deal. No! He wants to do anything he can to avoid this tragedy. What does he do? (He falls down before the king, begs him to be patient, and he will pay all that is owed.) Can this servant deliver on his promise of paying all? (No!) Even if he worked hard for the rest of his life, he would never be able to pay such a huge amount in full. This servant is begging the king for mercy. What does "mercy" mean? Mercy is not receiving what we do deserve; it is compassion for one who is miserable. The servant is a miserable man. He clearly owes an enormous debt to the king, and the king has every right to sell the servant and his family into slavery to help pay part of the debt. But the servant is hoping to change the king's mind and avoid such a terrible fate. He begs for mercy.

Read Matthew 18:27. How did the king react to the servant who begged for mercy? (He was moved with compassion.) We talked about compassion in Lesson 2, the Good Samaritan. Do you remember what "compassion" means? (Compassion is pity, sympathy, or suffering with another.) Compassion moves someone to act and do something to help. What did the compassion of the king cause him to do for the servant? (He forgave the debt.) This is huge! In one brief order from the king, this servant's whole life was just changed. No longer is he facing slavery and the slavery and separation of his entire family. No longer is he in danger of losing his home and everything he owns. No longer does he have the weight of a huge debt on his shoulders. He is free.

Read Matthew 18:28-30. What would be the first thing you would do if you were the servant and the king had just forgiven your debt? (Answers will vary.) I'm not sure what I would do first – jump for joy, run home to my family, shout the wonderful news to my friends, thank the king... Yet this servant didn't do any of those things. What did he immediately do? (He went looking for someone who owed him some money.) He found a fellow servant who owed him one hundred denarii. This would have been about how much a common laborer would have earned in one hundred days or about three months of working. It was a few dollars and absolutely nothing compared to the debt of ten thousand talents which could never have been repaid. How did he "request" the payment of the debt? (He grabbed the fellow servant by the throat and demanded full payment.) He doesn't just ask for the money, he demands it and with violence. He grabs the man by the throat! How did the fellow servant react? (He begged him for patience and time to pay the debt in full.) If this man was given enough time, could he have paid this debt of one hundred denarii? More than likely, yes! It was not a huge amount of money by any stretch. But was the servant willing to wait for the money that was owed him? Absolutely not! Isn't it interesting that this fellow servant does and says the same thing that the first servant did and said to the king? He falls down at his feet and begs for mercy. When the servant saw this man at his feet and heard him saying the same words he himself had said to the king just a short while before, it should have softened his heart and moved him with compassion. Sadly, the one who was shown so much mercy is not going to be one bit merciful. What did he do to his fellow servant when he could not pay him? (He had him thrown into prison until he could pay the debt.) How would he be able to work to repay the debt if he's locked up in a prison? It's not likely that he could. This shows how cruel and heartless this man was.

Read Matthew 18:31. Was this done in secret or did others know about it? (Others knew) Some fellow servants knew exactly what had happened to the poor servant, and they were very upset at his treatment by their fellow servant. They have compassion on him and go to the one person who can do something to help him. Whom did they go to? (The king)

Read Matthew 18:32-33. The king calls the unforgiving servant to him. If you were the unforgiving servant who had been forgiven so much by the king, then cruelly refused to show mercy and forgiveness to another and now are being summoned by the king for your behavior, how would you feel? What does the king call him? (A wicked servant) To be a wicked person is to do evil things. He was called wicked because he refused to be compassionate and forgiving to another. He was expected to show mercy to others, especially after he was shown so much mercy by the king. He was not thankful for what he had received when he should have had a heart overflowing with gratitude. A wicked servant. There will now be severe consequences for his heartless actions.

Read Matthew 18:34-35. The king was very angry and ordered a harsh punishment for this servant. What was it? (The servant was to be delivered to the torturers until the debt could be paid.) At this point, the original command of slavery and selling all the possessions probably looked pretty good compared to what he faced now. There is no hope of the debt ever being paid so his imprisonment and torture will last the rest of his life. Does the man deserve this? Is the king being too severe? **James 2:13** begins, *"For judgment is without mercy to the one who has shown no mercy."* Remember why Jesus told this parable? Peter was asking him about forgiveness. Jesus wanted Peter (and us) to see some very important truths: 1) The king represents God, and God is merciful to those who seek His mercy. 2) God forgives our debt of sin, which is one we could never repay. 3) The wrongs that others do to us are nothing compared to the wrong we have done to God through our sin. 4) We should be so grateful for the blessing of God's forgiveness that it prompts us to always be forgiving to others. Jesus closes this parable with a warning: God will not forgive us if we are not willing to forgive others from our hearts. **Read Colossians 3:13.**

The parable of the unforgiving servant teaches us the importance of being merciful and forgiving to others, and it reminds us to always be thankful for the mercy and forgiveness that God shows us.

Review Questions: (Answers are provided in the Answer Key.)

1. Up to how many times was Peter willing to forgive others?

2. How many times did Jesus say Peter should be willing to forgive?

3. What did Jesus mean by that number?

4. How much did the servant who could not pay owe the king?

5. What did the king originally propose to help settle the debt?

6. How did the servant respond to the king's original command?

7. What did the servant promise the king that he would never be able to do?

8. When the king was moved with compassion, what did he do to help the servant?

9. What was the first thing the servant did after being released by the king?

10. What was interesting about what the fellow servant did and said?

11. What was done to the fellow servant who could not pay his debt?

12. Who told the king what the unforgiving servant had done?

13. How did the king refer to the unforgiving servant?

14. What punishment was ordered by the king?

15. Will God forgive us if we are unwilling to forgive others?

 ## "Putting Down Roots": Memory Work

- Memorize Matthew 18:21-22

- Memorize Colossians 3:13

 ## "Add A Leaf": Words To Know

- Mercy

- Forgiveness

- Talents

 ## "Harvest Fun": Games & Activities

- Scripture Puzzle Race – This race will need two players or two teams. Before the race can begin, each team will need to write out Matthew 18:21-22 on a sheet of construction paper (one color per team). Turn the paper over and draw several random lines all over it. Cut along the lines to make puzzle pieces. Let someone who is not participating in the race hide all of the puzzle pieces around the room. When "Go" is called, let each team race to find all of the puzzle pieces in their color. Whichever team finds and correctly assembles all of their pieces first, wins. As a review, see how many players can say the verses from memory.

- Act it Out! - This would be a fun parable to act out. (Just don't literally choke the one servant too badly!) The characters would be: the king, the servant who owed more than he could ever pay, the servant who owed his fellow servant just a little, other fellow servants, and possibly the torturers?... Dress in costume if you'd like, but pay attention to the detail of this lesson. Notice that the king had great compassion, but the servant who was forgiven didn't seem grateful at all for the fact. Video this scene if you'd like or perform it in front of friends and family, then discuss the lessons we can all learn from this parable of Jesus.

- Group discussion – Have you ever found it hard to forgive? With your family or another group of people, discuss different situations that are/were hard to forgive. Why is it sometimes so hard to let go of hard feelings? How can we use scripture to help us with that? What are some good scriptures to memorize about forgiveness? How does looking at Jesus' willingness to forgive us help us to forgive others?

"Digging Deeper": Research

- Servitude for debt – Being sold as a slave (or having your family sold) was an option that could have been used against you in ancient times if you had debts you could not pay. Read the following scriptures about this topic, then do some further research and write down what you learn: II Kings 4:1; Leviticus 25:39-41; Exodus 22:2-3.

- Forgiveness – The Bible is filled with numerous examples of forgiveness. Sometimes, we see extraordinary examples of someone forgiving a very grievous wrong. Look up the following scriptures, then fill in the appropriate information on a chart in your notebook. Scriptures: 1) Genesis 37:3-4,19-28; 45:1-15, 2) Numbers 12:1-13, 3) II Samuel 16:5-6; 19:18-23, 4) I Kings 1:5-18, 43-53, 5) Luke 23:26-38, 6) Acts 6:9-15; 7:55-60, 7) II Timothy 1:1; 4:16-17 Chart: Column #1 – Who was wronged, Column #2 – Who wronged them, Column #3 – How they were wronged, Column #4 – Response of the one who was wronged.

"Food For Thought": Puzzles

- True or False – Read each statement below and decide if it is true or false. Write the correct answer on the line. Answers are provided in the Answer Key.

_____ 1. Peter asked Jesus if he should forgive others up to seven times.

_____ 2. Jesus answered Peter that he should forgive forty-nine times.

_____ 3. A certain servant owed the king 20,000 talents.

_____ 4. The king commanded the servant who owed much and his family be sold.

_____ 5. The servant who owed much agreed to he and his family becoming slaves.

_____ 6. The king showed mercy and forgave the huge debt of the servant.

_____ 7. The servant whose debt was forgiven, immediately demanded he be paid what little was owed him by a fellow servant.

_____ 8. Many fellow servants cheered him on for throwing the debtor in prison.

_____ 9. The king was extremely angry at the unmerciful servant.

_____ 10. The king had the unmerciful servant executed for his lack of compassion.

- Matching – Match the following scriptures about forgiveness with the correct reference. Answers are provided in the Answer Key.

_____ 1. "I, even I am He who blots out your transgressions for My own sake..."   a. Luke 17:3

_____ 2. "For I will forgive their iniquity, and their sin I will remember no more."   b. Psalm 86:5

_____ 3. "And be kind to one another, tenderhearted, forgiving one another, just as God in Christ also forgave you."   c. Matthew 6:14

_____ 4. "Then Jesus said, 'Father, forgive them, for they do not know what they do.'"   d. Isaiah 43:25

_____ 5. "For You, Lord, are good, and ready to forgive, and abundant in mercy to all those who call upon You."

e. Colossians 3:13

_____ 6. "For this is My blood of the new covenant, which is shed for many for the remission of sins."

f. Matthew 18:21

_____ 7. "Then Peter came to Him and said, 'Lord, how often shall my brother sin against me, and I forgive him...'"

g. Jeremiah 31:34

_____ 8. "Take heed to yourselves. If your brother sins against you, rebuke him; and if he repents, forgive him."

h. Ephesians 4:32

_____ 9. "Bearing with one another, and forgiving one another... even as Christ forgave you, so you also must do."

i. Matthew 26:28

_____ 10. "For if you forgive men their trespasses, your heavenly Father will also forgive you."

j. Luke 23:34

"Fruits Of Our Labor": Crafts

• Wipe the slate clean! - For this craft, you will be making your own chalkboard. You can use it for all kinds of cool stuff, but while you are doing this study, you can use it to write your memory verse for the week. It is also a good reminder that forgiveness helps us to "wipe the slate clean." For this craft you will need: A "board" which can be a clipboard, a dollar store platter, a picture frame, etc.; chalkboard paint; and acrylic paint in a color of your choice (optional). To begin, if you want a colored border around your chalkboard, you will need to cover and tape over the area that will be painted with chalkboard paint. Paint your exposed border with an acrylic paint color of your choice. Let it dry completely. Next, you will need to cover and tape off the painted border. Now you are ready to use your chalkboard paint. Chalkboard paint comes in liquid or spray. If using spray, spray one coat of chalkboard paint and let it dry. Repeat with a second layer. If using liquid, spread the paint on your surface with a sponge applicator or a small paint roller. You can use a paintbrush, but it will probably leave lines or ridges on your chalkboard. Once the paint is dry, you're ready to hang or display your chalkboard wherever you'd like. (Don't forget to purchase some chalk and an eraser!)

- Design a crown - There have been many types of crowns throughout history, some very simple ones using items from nature and others very elaborate and expensive. If you were a king (or queen) and could wear a crown, what would you want it to look like? Try your hand at designing a crown. Think about the shape you would like, any favorite colors and any items you would like to incorporate. Do you like the thought of a leafy vine woven around your head? Or do you like the thought of glittering jewels? Be creative and original with your design! For even more fun, do this activity with some friends and compare crowns when everyone is finished. Do any two look exactly alike?

- Illustrate a parable - Illustrate the parable from this lesson. You can continue the same method you have been using or choose a different way to illustrate it.

Lesson 5: Parable of the Talents

Text: Matthew 25:14-30

"Growing In The Word": Lesson Text & Discussion

Read Matthew 25:14-15. In our last lesson, we talked about what a talent was and its great value. Keep that in mind as we discuss this parable. A wealthy man was preparing to go on a long journey so he called his servants to him in order to divide his goods among them while he was away. He was trusting them with a big responsibility by putting his money in their hands. How many servants did the man have and what did he give to each of them? (He had three servants. To one he gave five talents, to another he gave two talents and to the third one he gave one talent.) Notice that each of the servants received something although it was not the same amount. Even though one of the servants only received one talent, that was still a very valuable sum! The master knew the abilities of each of his servants and expected them to use them in handling his wealth. He didn't give any of them more than he thought they could handle.

Read Matthew 25:16-18. Two of the servants got to work immediately. They used their talents wisely and made more of a profit for their master. How much did the five-talent man increase his share by? (He increased his share by five more talents.) How much did the two-talent man increase his share by? (He increased his share by two talents more.) So two of the servants doubled the amount of money they were responsible for. They were successful because they worked hard. The one-talent man did something a little strange with his master's money. What was it? (He buried it in the ground.) We will read about his explanation for this later, but do you have any thoughts as to why he did this? (Answers will vary.) This servant was afraid to try, afraid to work, and afraid to put forth any effort so he took the easy way out and did nothing with his master's money except to stick it in the ground.

Read Matthew 25:19-23. The master was gone for quite a long time, but as soon as he came back, he called his servants to come before him to settle their accounts. He wanted to know what his servants had been doing and if they had been faithful during his absence. What does it mean to be faithful? (To be faithful means to be loyal and true. It is to be dependable to do everything that is expected and required of you.) The master called the five-talent man before him first and then the two-talent man. Both of these servants reported what they had accomplished. The master was very pleased and praised them. How did he refer to them? (He called them good and faithful servants.) He praised them for being trustworthy and hardworking, and he wanted to reward them for being good servants. In what two ways does he do this? (1-He tells the servants he will make them ruler over many things because they were faithful over a few. 2-They're also invited to enter into the joy of their lord.) These servants were going to be given even more than they had before, and they were going to enjoy the privilege of being in their master's presence, not as servants but as invited guests or companions.

Read Matthew 25:24-25. Now the one-talent man appears before his master. How does this servant refer to his master? (He calls him a hard man.) He tells his master that he hid his talent because he was afraid of him. Was it reasonable for him to be afraid? (No) We did not see the other two servants reacting to the master in this way, and they had been entrusted with much more wealth than the one-talent man. If any of the servants had a reason to be fearful, it would have been the five-talent man who had the most of his master's money to lose! Even if his excuses sound somewhat believable, they are not the truth for his failure.

Read Matthew 25:26-27. Now the truth comes out! What does the master call this servant? (Wicked and lazy) Your Bible might use the word "slothful" which means lazy. **Read Proverbs 12:24.** Remember that one of the rewards for the five and two-talent servants was to be ruler over many things because they had been faithful over a few. They were hard workers and proved what this proverb says, *"The hand of the diligent will rule."* What is the opposite of being diligent? (Lazy or slothful) This was one of the one-talent man's problems – he was lazy. He was unwilling to work, unwilling to put forth any effort on behalf of his master, unwilling to show himself a faithful servant. The master knew the truth but said that even if his excuses had been right, if he was a cruel master that his servant should have been afraid of, then what was the easiest thing the servant should have at least done with the one talent? (He should have put it in the bank.) If the servant had at least done this, the master's money would have gained a little bit of interest (or usury) at the bank, and there would have been a little profit made.

Read Matthew 25:28-29. What did the master order to be done? (He ordered that the one talent be taken from the wicked and lazy servant and given to the man with ten talents.) There's a saying that goes, "If you don't use it, you lose it!" The wicked, lazy servant wasn't responsible or faithful enough to take care of what he'd been trusted with so it was taken from him and given to the one who was the most faithful and trustworthy.

Read Matthew 25:30. How is the servant referred to in this verse? (He is called "unprofitable.") To be unprofitable is to be completely useless. Just as the other two servants were rewarded for their efforts, this servant is punished for making no effort at all. What was his punishment? (He was to be cast into outer darkness.) He would no longer be in the presence of his master. He was shut out forever.

At the beginning of this parable, Jesus compares the kingdom of heaven to this wealthy master and his servants. The master represents God. He gives each of us "talents" according to our abilities, to what we can handle. We don't all get the same thing, but we each get something that we can use in service to God, and we are expected to be faithful in using them to God's glory. When we are profitable servants and being useful for God in His kingdom, He will continue to bless us with more because He knows we can handle more and use it responsibly. But if we fail to use what He has given us, we can lose it. Let's work hard to be faithful servants in God's kingdom so that one day we can hear the words, *"Enter into the joy of your Lord."*

Review Questions: (Answers are provided in the Answer Key.)

1. In the parable of the talents, how many servants did the man have and what did he give to each one of them before traveling on his journey?

2. How did the master decide how much to trust each servant with?

3. How many of the servants increased their share of their master's money?

4. What did the one-talent servant do with his share of his master's money?

5. How did the master refer to the five and two-talent servants?

6. What two rewards does the master give to these servants?

7. How did the one-talent man refer to his master?

8. Was this true about the master?

9. What did the master call the one-talent man?

10. What does Proverbs 12:24 tell us that the hand of the diligent will do?

11. What was the easiest thing the one-talent man should have at least done with the master's money?

12. What did the master order to be done with the one-talent man's talent?

13. Who was it given to?

14. What was the one-talent man's punishment?

15. How does the master refer to this servant as his punishment is announced?

"Putting Down Roots": Memory Work

- Memorize Matthew 25:21

- Memorize I Corinthians 4:1-2

- Memorize Proverbs 12:24

"Add A Leaf": Words To Know

- Faithful

- Slothful

- Usury

- Unprofitable

"Harvest Fun": Games & Activities

- Hide the Talent! - Use the talent template located in Appendix B in the back of this book to play this game. Make a copy of the talent template page and cut one talent out. To make it sturdier, copy onto card stock and/or laminate it. Let someone hide the talent, then let others try to find it. The hider can use "hot or cold" clues if desired. When one finds the hidden talent, he may hide it next so play can continue. After the game is finished, discuss the one talent man in the parable. Why did he hide the one talent he was given? Was it right or wrong of him to do this and why?

- Use Your Talents Wisely – Make several copies of the talent template page located in Appendix B. (You may want to laminate these for sturdiness.) Cut them apart and distribute three talents to each player at the beginning of this activity. Players will gain or lose talents by how they answer the scenarios given to them. If they answer wisely, they gain a talent, if they don't answer wisely or can't answer at all, they lose a talent. Play until one player reaches 10 talents or as long as you would like. (You could also ask lesson questions for review instead of the scenarios.) Make up different scenarios and write them down on index cards or use "Kid's Choices" pocket card game found online or at Christian bookstores. (This card set has dilemmas for ages 6-11 that must be solved using Biblical principles. The cards cost around $6.00.) Some examples might include: 1) You got a new bike for Christmas and your friend wants to ride on it. You let your friend ride it and they accidentally run over a nail in the street and flatten the tire. What do you do? 2) While standing in line at the movies, someone cuts in front of you. What do you say? 3) You received some unexpected birthday money that will finally give you enough to buy something you've been wanting for a long time, but then it is announced at church that a missionary will be visiting the following week and really needs funds to help spread the gospel. What will you do with your birthday money?

 ## "Digging Deeper": Research

- Talents – The talents in this parable were not abilities but measurements of money. What exactly was a talent? What different kinds of metal could a talent be? Were talents of great or little value? Did talents have a constant or fluctuating value?

- Biblical currency - Paper money was invented by the Chinese but not until the 12th century, so what kinds of money were used in Bible times? Do some research into Biblical currency (money). What was the barter system and what items were bartered? What metals were used for payment and what weights/measurements did they come in? Who first invented coins and what did they look like? Did the Jews have any coins of their own?

"Food For Thought": Puzzles

• What's Missing? - Fill in the missing words of the verses below, and write the correct reference in the parentheses. Answers are provided in the Answer Key.

Matthew 25:15   Matthew 25:20

Matthew 25:23   Matthew 25:25   Matthew 25:29

---

1. "And I was _____, and went and _____ your _____ in the _____. Look, there you have what is _____." (   )

2. "And to one he gave _____ talents, to another _____, and to another _____, to each according to his own _____; and immediately he went on a _____." (   )

3. "For to _____ who has, _____ will be given, and he will have _____; but from him who does not _____, even what he _____ will be _____ _____." (   )

4. "So he who had received _____ talents came and brought _____ other talents, saying, 'Lord, you delivered to me _____ talents; look, I have gained _____ more talents beside them.'" (   )

5. "His _____ said to him, 'Well done, good and _____ servant; you have been _____ over a _____ things, I will make you _____ over _____ things. Enter into the _____ of your _____.'" (   )

- Acrostic – Use the letters of the word "talents" to make words that describe ways to faithfully serve the Lord. For example, for the first letter T, you could write the word "totally" or the word "trusting." Answers will vary.

T

A

L

E

N

T

S

 "Fruits Of Our Labor": Crafts

- Biblical coins – For this craft you will need Sculpey clay in "coin" colors such as gold, silver or tan. You will also need a carving tool such as a toothpick. If you did the research project on Biblical currency, then you have probably seen several different types of coins that were used in Bible times. If not, search the Internet (with supervision) or an illustrated Bible encyclopedia for some pictures of biblical coins to use as models for this craft. Try sculpting a Jewish coin such as a mite, a Greek coin such as a drachma, and a Roman coin such as a denarius plus any others you would like. When you are finished sculpting and carving your coins, they can be baked to harden if you so choose. Sculpey clay needs to be baked at 275 degrees for 15 minutes per 1/4 inch of thickness.

- Illustrate a parable - Illustrate the parable from this lesson. You can continue the same method you have been using or choose a different way to illustrate it.

Lesson 6: Parables of the Persistent Friend & the Persistent Woman and the Judge

Text: Luke 11:5-10; 18:1-8

"Growing In The Word": Lesson Text & Discussion

Read Luke 11:5-7. In the first four verses of this chapter, Jesus was teaching his disciples how to pray. We commonly call this "the Lord's Prayer." Immediately after this, Jesus begins to teach an interesting parable. He asks his disciples to imagine a scene where they have a problem – an unexpected visitor has arrived and they have no food to offer their guest. What does Jesus suggest they would do in that situation? (They would go to a friend or neighbor's house and ask to borrow bread.) To make the scene even more complicated, what time does he say they would go and ask to borrow bread? (Midnight) All of this would be an embarrassing scene! First, it would be embarrassing to have a guest show up at your house, and you have no food. Second, it would be embarrassing to have to wake up your friend in the middle of the night to borrow food from him. But despite the embarrassment, Jesus makes the point to his disciples that they would do whatever they had to in order to get some food for their guest. How many loaves of bread would they ask to borrow? (Three) What was the sleeping friend's reply? (Leave me alone!) At first, the sleeping friend seems annoyed. It's very late at night, all of his household is asleep, and he really doesn't want to have to climb out of his comfortable bed and get up to answer the door! End of story? Not quite.

Read Luke 11:8. Jesus finishes the parable by showing the disciples that if they were persistent, the sleepy friend would get up and give them as much food as was needed. What does it mean to be persistent? Persistence is the ability to stick with something. It means you don't give up; you keep trying. In this parable, the man who needed to borrow bread didn't just ask once then give up and go home when the first answer he received was "No." He continued to knock, he continued to ask and plead with his friend to help him until the answer was finally "Yes." Persistence paid off.

Read Luke 11:9-10. Now Jesus gets down to the heart of what this parable means. He is talking about being persistent in prayer. God has three answers to our prayers: yes, no, not right now (wait). Sometimes, we pray for something once and the answer seems to be no. But what might happen if we persist in prayer? What does Jesus tell us to do in verse 9? (Ask, seek, and knock) The desperate man didn't receive the needed bread the first time he asked for it. He had to keep asking. Jesus was telling his disciples (and is telling us) to be persistent in our prayers.

Read Luke 18:1-3. Just a few chapters after the last parable, Jesus again is teaching a parable about persistence in prayer. How often does he say people should pray? (Always) **I Thessalonians 5:17** reminds us to *"pray without ceasing."* Jesus is also stressing persistence as he reminds us not to lose heart. Don't give up! Keep praying! He begins this parable by introducing its two main characters. Who are they? (A judge and a widow) Would you describe this judge as a good man? Why or why not? This man did not care about God or other people which means he did not do his job as judge with a heart full of compassion. He just didn't care. What did the widow want this judge to do for her? (She wanted him to avenge her of her adversary.) First of all, what is an adversary? An adversary is an enemy or someone who is against us. The widow apparently had been wronged by someone, and she had suffered a great injustice. She wanted the judge to avenge it for her. To avenge is to harm or punish someone who has harmed or wronged you in some way. Many widows had a very difficult time in Bible times. If they had no children to take care of them and provide for them, they were often very poor and struggled to survive. This widow may have suffered the loss of something that she absolutely couldn't afford to lose. She knew the judge was a man of authority who could do something about it, so she went to him and demanded justice!

Read Luke 18:4-5. Was the judge moved with pity for this poor widow? (No) At first, he didn't consider her case at all. What finally changed his mind? (The persistence of the widow) The widow didn't give up after asking the judge for justice once. This matter was too important to her to just let it go. She kept after him and after him, determined to keep on until he decided to help her. At last, he made up his mind to rule in her favor and grant her justice just so she would stop bothering him! But just like the first parable, we see that persistence paid off.

Read Luke 18:6-8. Is God like the judge in this parable? (No) God loves us and is always moved with compassion when he sees we are mistreated and hurting. He isn't bored or uncaring like the judge was, but rather, He is ready to avenge us speedily. God desires to help us and wants us to come to Him with our troubles. We don't ever have to wonder *if* God will listen, *if* God will care, or *if* God will help. God is faithful. What question does Jesus ask at the end of the parable concerning all of us? (Will he find faith on the earth?) We know God is faithful; He is expecting us to be faithful to Him. One of the ways we can do that is to be a people of prayer and to be persistent in praying to Him about things that are very important to us.

Remember the three ways God answers our prayers? (Yes, no, wait) Part of having faith in God when we pray to Him is to realize that He always knows what is best for us and will give the right answer to each and every prayer.

<u>Review Questions</u>: (Answers are provided in the Answer Key.)

1. What was Jesus teaching his disciples about in the first four verses of Luke 11?

2. What time of night was the scene of the parable set?

3. What was the problem in this parable?

4. How many loaves of bread did the man ask to borrow from his friend?

5. Why did the friend say "No" at first?

6. Why was the man successful in borrowing bread from his friend?

7. What are three ways God answers our prayers?

8. According to Jesus, how often should we pray?

9. Who were the two main characters in the second parable?

10. Describe the judge.

11. What did the widow want the judge to do for her?

12. Was the judge moved with pity by the widow's case?

13. What made the judge finally decide to rule in her favor?

14. Is God like the judge in this parable?

15. How does God avenge His own people?

16. What does Jesus want to find on the earth when he comes again one day?

17. Will you be faithful to God?

 "Putting Down Roots": Memory Work

- Memorize Luke 11:9-10

- Memorize Luke 18:1

"Add A Leaf": Words To Know

- Persistence

- Avenge

- Adversary

"Harvest Fun": Games & Activities

- "Lend me three loaves!" - The object of this game is to be the first player or team to acquire three loaves of bread. Before play begins, make several copies of the loaf of bread template in Appendix B onto card stock and/or laminate them. In order for a player or team to receive a loaf, a question needs to be answered correctly. Questions may come from this lesson and include memory work and "Add a leaf" word definitions if desired, or this would also be a good opportunity to review the first five lessons in this study by asking review questions from those lessons. The first player or team to get three loaves wins. To make it more challenging, award points for each correct answer, then award one loaf of bread in point increments such as at 5 points, 10 points, etc.

- Prayer Journal - I Thessalonians 5:17 tells us to "pray without ceasing." There are so many people who need us to pray for them, and we need to be persistent in "asking, seeking, and knocking." We can pray for those who are sick, those who are sad, those in leadership both of the church and our nation, missionaries, soldiers... Start a prayer journal where you can write down the names of the people you want to pray for and the date of the prayer request or date that you first started praying for them. Write down any answers you see to your prayers such as someone getting well or finding a job. It is so encouraging to look back through your prayer journal after several months and see how God has answered different prayers. (Instructions to make your own prayer journal are in the crafts section of this lesson, or you can purchase a blank journal from a store.)

- Sharing Bread – One neighbor was willing to share three loaves of bread with his persistent friend. May we always be willing to share food with those who are in need. Try your hand at making one of the following quick bread recipes, then think about someone you could share the bread with. Do you know anyone who is hungry? Do you know anyone who is lonely? Do you know anyone who is tired or needs encouragement? Do you know anyone who has been busy in service to God?

Blueberry Tea Bread

2 cups all-purpose flour	1 tsp. grated orange peel (optional)
1 cup sugar	2 eggs
1 T. baking powder	1 cup milk
$\frac{1}{4}$ tsp. salt	3 T. cooking oil

1 $\frac{1}{2}$ cups fresh or frozen blueberries

In a bowl, combine the flour, sugar, baking powder and salt. Stir in blueberries and orange peel. In a separate bowl, beat eggs and add milk and oil. Stir into dry ingredients just until moistened. Do not overmix. Pour into a greased loaf pan. Bake at 350 degrees for 1 hour or until a toothpick inserted near the center comes out clean. Cool in pan for 10 minutes then remove to wire rack to cool completely.

Bacon & Cheddar Bread

6 slices bacon, cooked and crumbled	2 cups shredded cheddar cheese
2 cups all-purpose flour	1 cup milk
1 T. sugar	1 egg, beaten
1 $\frac{1}{2}$ tsp. baking powder	1 cup sour cream

1 tsp. salt   2 T. bacon drippings

½ tsp. pepper

In a large bowl, mix together the flour, sugar, baking powder, salt and pepper. Add in the bacon and cheese, stir to coat. In a separate bowl, combine the milk, egg, sour cream and bacon drippings. Stir into dry ingredients just until moistened. Spoon into a greased 9x5 loaf pan. Bake in a 375 degree oven for 40-45 minutes. Remove to a wire rack to cool completely.

 "Digging Deeper": Research

- Judges – The judge in the parable from this lesson was not a good one because he didn't fear God or care about people. Read the following scriptures to see what the Bible has to say about judges: Who could be a judge? What was expected of them, and what should they not do? Write down what you learn. (I Kings 3:9; Micah 7:3; Deuteronomy 16:18-20; I Kings 3:28) Find and list examples from the Bible of good and bad judges and why they are considered good or bad.

- Prayer – Prayer is powerful, and we are to take full advantage of it by being persistent in it. We read of many examples in the Bible of people praying. Some were praising God, others were asking for specific things for themselves while others were praying on behalf of someone else. It is interesting to look at some of these prayers to see the different things being prayed for as well as some of the different "prayer postures" people would use. By that, I mean some people would stand, some would kneel, etc. Read the following scriptures and note what the prayer request was and what prayer posture (if any) the person (or persons) were in: Ezra 9:5, 10:1; Exodus 34:8-9; I Chronicles 17:16-20; James 5:14-15; Nehemiah 9:5-6; Genesis 17:3; Luke 18:10-13.

"Food For Thought": Puzzles

- Who Said It? - Read the following quotations from the lesson, decide who said it, and write the answer on the line. Some answers may be used more than once. (All quotations are taken from the NKJV.) Answers are provided in the Answer Key.

1. "Ask, and it will be given to you; seek, and you will find; knock, and it will be opened to you." _____

2. "Friend, lend me three loaves." _____

3. "Do not trouble me; the door is now shut." _____

4. "Avenge me of my adversary." _____

5. "Hear what the unjust judge said." _____

6. "I do not fear God." _____

7. "Shall God not avenge His own elect who cry out day and night to Him?" _____

8. "I have nothing to set before him." _____

9. "My children are with me in bed; I cannot rise and give to you." _____

10. "Everyone who asks receives, and he who seeks finds, and to him who knocks it will be opened." _____

- Word Scramble - Read the following clues to help you unscramble the words. Answers are provided in the Answer Key.

1. This word describes someone who doesn't give up. t e n t r s p i e s _____

2. The one in this lesson was described as unjust. e j d u g _____

3. An enemy. v e y r a s d r a _____

4. It is how we talk to God. r a p y r e _____

5. This word describes a woman whose husband has died. d i w o w _____

6. To receive justice. g e v a n e _____

7. Someone who lives next door or nearby. g o r n h e b i _____

8. These are stories Jesus told the people to teach a spiritual meaning. b a r s p l a e

   _____

9. 12:00 a.m. g i t h i m n d _____

10. A man wanted to borrow three of these in bread. s l a v e o _____

"Fruits Of Our Labor": Crafts

- Prayer Journal - To make your own prayer journal, you will need two pieces of craft foam (same size), several sheets of lined or plain paper, a hole puncher, and yarn. First, cut or fold the paper to the size you want your journal to be. Next, cut the foam pieces about 1/2" larger than the paper. These will be the front and back covers of your journal. Use the hole puncher to punch three holes in the foam pieces and the paper. You need a hole near the top, a hole in the middle and one near the bottom. Each hole needs to be about 1/4" in from the edge. Assemble the journal by placing the paper inside the covers and lining up the holes. Use three pieces of yarn to tie the book together at each hole. Decorate the front of the journal any way you wish. You can use markers or foam letter stickers to spell out "Prayer Journal." Be as creative as you'd like with the cover. You may even want to write some scriptures about prayer on the cover or the first page such as I Thessalonians 5:17, James 5:16 or Mark 11:24.

- Bread loaf magnet - In one of the parables in this lesson, a man was persistently asking to borrow loaves of bread so he could offer food to his unexpected guests. For this craft you will need a sheet of brown craft foam, a sheet of white or tan craft foam, a fine point black sharpie pen, magnets, and wiggly eyes (optional). Use the loaf of bread template in Appendix B to cut out a bread loaf shape from the brown craft foam and a white or tan piece of foam for the cut bread in the front. Write the following Bible verse along the side of the bread shape: "Ask, and it will be given to you; seek, and you will find; knock, and it will be opened to you." (Luke 11:9) If you'd like, glue two wiggly eyes and draw a smile underneath on the front of your bread loaf. On the back of the bread shape, glue or stick magnets. Place your magnet on your refrigerator to remind you to be persistent in prayer.

- Illustrate a parable - Illustrate a parable from this lesson, or do both if you'd like. You can continue the same method you have been using or choose a different way to illustrate it.

Lesson 7: Parable of the Soils

Text: Luke 8:4-15

"Growing In The Word": Lesson Text & Discussion

Read Luke 8:4-7. As Jesus teaches the parable of the soils, who is he speaking to and how many of them are there? (He is speaking to a great crowd of people who had come from every city to hear him.) He has quite a large audience, and he is going to teach them a parable about something they would be very familiar with – farming. While very few people farm today, it was quite different in ancient times. Hundreds and thousands of years ago most people farmed or at least had some kind of garden because it was necessary. They couldn't run to the local grocery store to buy food anytime they wanted – they had to grow what they needed. Jesus begins this parable by talking about the farmer, or sower, going out to sow his seed. To do this, the farmer would usually carry a sack of seed under his arm, reach in for a handful of seed and throw it (or scatter it) along the ground as he walked along. "To sow" literally means "to scatter seed." A family member or servant would then follow along plowing the ground to cover the seed in the earth. But as the farmer sowed the seed, it became scattered in different places. In these verses, Jesus mentions three kinds of soil. What are they? (1-The wayside, 2-Rocky, 3- Soil with thorns) Were any of these three kinds of soil good places for the seed to fall? (No) The wayside was a foot path that people used as they traveled, and many fields ran right up to the edges of these trails. The dirt of this path would be hard as it was packed down from it being walked on so much. When some of the seed fell over the edges of the field and onto this path, it would get trampled down by people and animals walking over it. It became free bird food. The rocky soil was not soil that was full of rocks but a shallow layer of soil over a rocky ledge underneath it. The seed would have a little bit of soil to start growing in, but the roots couldn't go down very far before they hit the rocky ledge so the plants died soon after they sprouted. The soil containing thorns was able to hold the seed and let it grow, but the problem was it was sharing the ground with another kind of bad plant – the thorns which would grow with the good plants and choke them out so that they would die. None of these three kinds of soil were going to allow the farmer to reap a good harvest. But the parable continues...

Read Luke 8:8. What is the fourth kind of soil Jesus mentions? (The good soil) This is where the farmer will have success. His seed will go into this good soil and grow to produce a bountiful crop. How bountiful did Jesus say the harvest would yield? (A hundredfold) The "yield" is how much the land produced. In this case, the good soil yielded or produced a crop that was a hundred times as much as what was sown in seed. After finishing the parable, what did Jesus cry out to the crowd? (*"He who has ears to hear, let him hear!"*) Remember back in Lesson 1 we talked about how we sometimes hear, but we're not really listening? Jesus is strongly emphasizing again how important it is to really listen and pay attention to his teachings. We should not just let them go in one ear and out the other!

Read Luke 8:9-11. The disciples ask Jesus for an explanation. While it seems they are asking the meaning of the parable, what they are really asking him is why he speaks in parables. **Read Matthew 13:10-13.** Jesus says almost exactly the same thing in Luke 8 that he said in Matthew 13. You may remember we discussed this in Lesson 1. Do you remember why Jesus spoke to the people in parables? (Parables were going to serve two purposes: 1) They would reveal the mysteries of the kingdom. 2) They would conceal the mysteries of the kingdom.) Anyone who listened to the parables of Jesus could hear the words he spoke, but it was up to them if they were listening with a heart of faith. As Jesus begins to explain the meaning of the parable, what does he say the seed represents? (The Word of God) Just as seed is planted, God's Word must be planted in the hearts of people so that it can grow and bear fruit. Our hearts are like the soil, but not all hearts are "good ground." Jesus continues to explain...

Read Luke 8:12. Jesus explains the wayside soil. Who does he say comes and snatches the Word of God out of this kind of heart? (Satan) The wayside soil is a heart who hears the word but doesn't believe it and allow it to save him. Satan takes it away quickly just as the birds ate the seed that fell on the wayside.

Read Luke 8:13. Do the hearts that are like the rocky soil gladly receive the Word of God? (Yes) So what is their problem? (They have no root.) Just like the seed that fell on the rocky soil, these hearts hear and believe the Word of God for a little while, but they fall away quickly because they are shallow. They don't take time or make the effort to put down deep roots and grow. Instead the temptations of the world quickly distract them.

Read Luke 8:14. The hearts that are like the thorny ground also hear and believe the Word of God, but they let it get "choked out" by the thorns. What three things does Jesus say those thorns are? (1-Cares, 2-Riches, 3-Pleasures of life) These are believers who grow for a little while, but don't ever let their fruit ripen because one or all of the "thorns" grows up around them. The thorn of cares would be any kind of trouble or sorrow that a person would let overwhelm them and take them away from God and His Word. The riches and pleasures of life would be money, possessions, and fun things that one would let become more important in his life than God.

Read Luke 8:15. How does Jesus describe the heart that is like the good ground? (Noble and good) (Some versions may say "honest.") What does it mean to be noble? To be noble means to be righteous and virtuous. Someone who is noble has admirable personal qualities like honesty, generosity, etc. The heart that is like the good soil has all the right qualities for a successful crop. This heart wants to hear and obey the Word of God. This heart works hard to grow in the Lord and to bear good fruit for Him. How does one bear fruit for God? (Answers will vary.) There are many ways we can bear fruit for the Lord. **Read John 15:4.** We must stay close to the Lord (abide in Him) if we are to bear fruit. Can a branch broken off an apple tree keep growing apples on it? (No) Neither will we bear fruit if we disconnect ourselves from God and His Word. **Read Galatians 5:22-23.** There are a lot of "fruits" listed here that we are to put into practice if we have a heart of good soil. We can also bear fruit by serving others as God wants us to, and teaching the gospel to others. What does Jesus say we have to have as we bear fruit? (Patience) If you were to plant a tomato seed in the ground in your back yard today, would you be able to go out and pick a big, red, juicy tomato off of it tomorrow? (No) It takes time – a lot of time – for the seed to grow into a plant, then produce a little yellow flower out of which will grow a tiny green tomato that will continue to get bigger and riper and redder until it is finally ready to pick and be eaten. Farming and gardening take a lot of patience because one must wait for the harvest. It doesn't happen overnight. The heart of good soil realizes that following God faithfully requires perseverance. (You don't give up!)

What kind of soil are you? Is your heart made of good and noble soil, ready to hear God's Word and let it grow in your heart so you can bear a hundredfold of good fruit for Him? I pray that it is!

Review Questions: (Answers are provided in the Answer Key.)

1. What size crowd did Jesus teach this parable to?

2. How would a sower sow his seed in ancient times?

3. What does it mean "to sow"?

4. What were the four kinds of soil Jesus mentioned in this parable?

5. Which one of our five physical senses (seeing, hearing, smelling, tasting, touching) was Jesus emphasizing?

6. What did the seed represent in this parable?

7. Who snatches the soil out of the wayside heart?

8. What is the problem with the hearts that are like the rocky soil?

9. What are three things Jesus says the thorns represent?

10. How does Jesus describe the heart that is like the good ground?

11. How does one bear fruit for the Lord?

12. What kind of soil is your heart?

 ## "Putting Down Roots": Memory Work

- Memorize Luke 8:11

- Memorize Mark 4:20

- Memorize the four kinds of soil and what they represent: 1) Wayside – Hear the word but do not believe, 2) Rocky – Hear and believe but quickly fall away, 3) Thorny – Hear and believe but don't grow as they're choked with things of the world, 4) Good – Hear, believe and bear good fruit

 ## "Add A Leaf": Words To Know

- Yield

- Hundredfold

- Noble

 ## "Harvest Fun": Games & Activities

- Plant seeds – This activity goes along with one of the craft projects in this lesson. Choose some seeds for something you'd like to grow. You can grow fruits, vegetables, or even herbs. In order to be a successful gardener, there are some important things to remember: 1) Seeds need good soil! (Remember this from the parable?) If you live in an area (like me) where the soil isn't too good for growing things, buy some good potting soil to plant your seeds in. 2) Seeds need light and water so don't forget to water them, and plant them in an area where they will get the proper amount of sunlight. If you read the packet your seeds come in, it will tell you how much sun they need, how much water, and even how deep to plant the seeds. 3) Some seeds need to be planted deep while other need to be closer to the surface in order for the sunlight to reach them. Try starting out with some easier things to grow such as basil (an herb), squash, zucchini, or tomatoes. As you plant your seeds, think about the parable of the soils. The sower (the one doing the planting) wants to see his seeds grow and produce food. He will not want birds eating his seeds or weeds and thorns to kill his plants, or rocks and stones to prevent his plants from growing. Good soil is important for successful growth!

- Listening game – For this game, each player will need a paper plate (not styrofoam or slick-coated), a Sharpie marker, and good listening ears. The object of this game is to listen carefully to try to draw a picture that closely resembles what the teacher describes. To make it more challenging, players will not be able to look at their pictures as they're drawing. They must rely on what they are hearing. To begin, each player places their paper plate on top of their head. Then, as the teacher gives the following instructions, the players will carefully try to draw exactly what the teacher describes. At the conclusion, let everyone look at their picture to see how successful (or unsuccessful!) they were. (A scoring option is given at the end.) Drawing instructions: In the middle of the plate, draw a path representing the wayside. Draw dots for seed on the path. Draw some birds on the path. To the immediate left and right of the path, draw some lines to make square patches of fields. In one of the squares, draw rocks to represent the rocky soil. In another square, draw thorny plants. In another square, draw good crops. Scoring option: Score 1 point for the path. Score 2 points if seeds are drawn inside the path. Score 1 point if some are on the path and some are outside of it. Score 3 points for every bird drawn. Score 2 points for each square of field. Score 5 points for every rock drawn. Score 2 points for every thorny plant. Score 2 points for every good plant drawn. Score 3 points each for every fruit or vegetable drawn on the good plants. Add up the scores to see who has the most points.

"Digging Deeper": Research

• Agriculture in the Bible – Farming dates back all the way to the garden of Eden when Adam was told by God to look after the garden. (Genesis 2:15) Do some research into farming in the Bible. How many agricultural seasons was Israel's year divided into? What kind of crops did they grow? How did they plow the land? Did they only harvest once a year? What was involved in threshing and winnowing? How would it affect a family if a crop failed? Can you see how important it would be for a farmer to sow his seed in the best kind of soil?

• Ears – Research the fascinating intricacies of our ears and how we hear. Did you know that the middle ear contains the tiniest bone in our bodies? What is it called and what does it look like?

 ## "Food For Thought": Puzzles

• Coded Message – Use the key to break the code. Answer is provided in the Answer Key.

| ___ | ___ | ___ | | ___ | ___ | ___ | | ___ | ___ | ___ | ___ | | ___ | ___ | ___ | ___ |
| 25 | 6 | 7 | | 7 | 19 | 22 | | 12 | 13 | 22 | 8 | | 7 | 19 | 26 | 7 |

| ___ | ___ | ___ | ___ | | ___ | ___ | | ___ | ___ | ___ | | ___ | ___ | ___ | ___ |
| 21 | 22 | 15 | 15 | | 12 | 13 | | 7 | 19 | 22 | | 20 | 12 | 12 | 23 |

_ _ _ _ _ _   _ _ _   _ _ _ _ _
GROUND ARE THOSE

_ _ _,   _ _ _ _ _ _   _ _ _ _ _
WHO HAVING HEARD

_ _ _   _ _ _ _   _ _ _ _   _
THE WORD WITH A

_ _ _ _ _   _ _ _   _ _ _ _
NOBLE AND GOOD

_ _ _ _ _,   _ _ _ _   _ _   _ _ _
HEART KEEP IT AND

_ _ _ _   _ _ _ _ _   _ _ _ _
BEAR FRUIT WITH

_ _ _ _ _ _ _ _.   (_ _ _ _ 8:15)
PATIENCE LUKE

Key to the Code:

F N R U A G O S V C H T D I E B W K Y P M L J
21 13 9 6 26 20 12 8 5 24 19 7 23 18 22 25 4 16 2 11 14 15 17

Growing Up in God's Word: Parables of Jesus

Page 68   © 2017, Pryor Convictions Media, Paul & Heather Pryor, St. Petersburg, FL

- Sequence - Put the following quotations of Jesus from this lesson in the proper order, numbering them from 1-10. Answers are provided in the Answer Key.

_____ 1. "But the ones on the rock are those who, when they hear, receive the word with joy; and these have no root, who believe for a while and in time of temptation fall away."

_____ 2. "Some fell on rock; and as soon as it sprang up it withered away because it lacked moisture."

_____ 3. "He who has ears to hear, let him hear!"

_____ 4. "But others fell on good ground, sprang up and yielded a crop a hundredfold."

_____ 5. "A sower went out to sow his seed."

_____ 6. "But the ones that fell on the good ground are those who, having heard the word with a noble and good heart, keep it and bear fruit with patience."

_____ 7. "And some fell among thorns, and the thorns sprang up with it and choked it."

_____ 8. "The ones that fell among thorns are those who, when they have heard, go out and are choked with cares, riches, and pleasures of life, and bring no fruit to maturity."

_____ 9. "And as he sowed, some seed fell by the wayside; and it was trampled down, and the birds of the air devoured it."

_____ 10. "Those by the wayside are the ones who hear; then the devil comes and takes away the word out of their hearts, lest they should believe and be saved."

"Fruits Of Our Labor": Crafts

- Garden Markers - For this craft, you will create some plant markers for your herb/vegetable garden you planted from the Activities section. Once you plant your seeds, it is important to put a little plant stake or marker in that row or spot so you remember what plants will come up in that location. Write the name of the plant on an index card or piece of card stock. Once your cards are done and decorated as you like, laminate them or seal them inside contact paper to waterproof them. Nail them to a small wooden stake and push the stake into the soil in the proper location. If you have scrap pieces of wood, you can paint those instead of using cards.

- Fruits of the Spirit tree – When the word of God takes root in our hearts and grows, it will produce fruits of the Spirit in our lives. We can find a list of these fruits in Galatians 5:22-23. Turn to that passage of scripture and count how many fruits there are. Then, make a fruits of the Spirit tree to remind you to grow those fruits in your life. You can make the tree anyway you'd like. You might want to find some branches in your yard, place them in a tall vase or container, then make fruits you can attach to the branches. Or you can draw a huge tree with branches on brown butcher paper, cut it out and tape it to the wall. Make fruits to attach to the branches. Make sure the fruits are labeled such as "gentleness", "love", etc. You might want to start with placing just one fruit on your tree, then spend a week focusing on growing that fruit. Continue to add one new fruit each week. Be creative!

- Illustrate a parable - Illustrate the parable from this lesson. You can continue the same method you have been using or choose a different way to illustrate it.

Lesson 8: Parable of the Two Sons

Text: Matthew 21:28-32

"Growing In The Word": Lesson Text & Discussion

Read Matthew 21:28. How many sons did the man in this parable have? (Two) In this verse, he only speaks to one son, but what he says will be repeated to the second son as well. If you have studied grammar in school, you may remember that there are four kinds of sentences: a statement, a command or request, an exclamation, and a question. Did the father ask his sons to do something or did he give them a command to do something? (He gave them a command.) What did the father want his sons to do? (He wanted them to go and work in his vineyard.) Notice that the father didn't *ask* his sons if they wanted to go and work, or if they felt like working that day, or if they had some spare time it would be great if they could pitch in. There was work to be done and the father needed his sons to do it. When did the father want the work to be done? (That day) The father said, "Go work *today* in my vineyard. This wasn't work that could wait until later when they had some extra time or felt like doing it. It was urgent work that needed to be done immediately.

Read Matthew 21:29. What was the response of the first son? (He told his father he wouldn't go.) How would you describe the way this son answered his father? (Answers will vary.) This son was being disrespectful and disobedient at first. As a son, he should have been submitting to the authority of his father. There should have been no question whether he should have obeyed him or not. Do you ever find it hard to obey? Are there times when you're asked to do something that you really don't feel like doing? Maybe you've even acted as this first son did – maybe you've said, "I will not!" But that wasn't the end of his response, was it? How did he feel later on? (He regretted the way he had answered his father and obediently went to work.) Can you think of any example in the Bible of someone who didn't want to obey the Lord at first but then was sorry later and obeyed what he was told to do? (Answers will vary but may include Moses when God spoke to him at the burning bush, Jonah, Naaman, King Manasseh...) What this young man did was repent. Do you remember how we learned about repentance in the parable of the prodigal son? What does it mean to repent? (Repentance is being sorry for sin, but then changing your life.) When this son felt sorrow and regret over the way he had answered his father, he made changes. He got up and went to work. He obeyed.

Read Matthew 21:30. Now the father gives the same command to his second son. How did he answer his father? (He said, "I go, sir.") This son gave a polite, respectful answer that indicated he was going to obey, but what was the problem? (He didn't go to work!)

Would you say that this son was being obedient to his father? (No!) Just saying words was not getting the job done. What if your mother asked you to wash the dishes and you cheerfully answered, "Sure, mom, I'll be happy to!", but then you go outside and play for awhile, then come in and read a book, then get a snack from the kitchen, then go to a movie with a friend? Did the dishes get washed just because you happily said you would do the chore? No! This son needed to take action and actually *do* what his father wanted him to do.

Read Matthew 21:31. What question does Jesus ask the people he was teaching this parable to? ("*Which of the two did the will of his father?*") The answer to the question Jesus asked the crowd was obvious – the first son is the one who did his father's will; he did the work his father wanted him to do. With the story over, Jesus begins to explain the meaning of this parable to his listeners. Who do you think is like the father in the parable? (God) The father represents God and the two sons represent two kinds of people: 1) Those who were unbelievers and rebellious toward God but then believed, repented and obeyed him faithfully. 2) Those who claimed to be faithful believers and seemed righteous but did not do what God wanted them to do. We learn from verse 23 of this chapter to whom Jesus told this parable. Who were they? (The chief priests and elders of the people) These would have been the religious leaders of the Jews at that time. These also would have been the kind of people who would have described themselves as faithful to God, ones were righteous and pure. But! Who did Jesus say would enter the kingdom of heaven before them? (Tax collectors and harlots) **Read Matthew 7:21.** In this verse, who does Jesus say will enter the kingdom of heaven? (Those who do the will of the Father) The Jews (and in particular their religious leaders) couldn't stand tax collectors. They thought of them as liars, cheats, and thieves. They also couldn't stand harlots. These were women of bad reputation who did things with men that only married women should do with their husbands. The "righteous" Jews considered these two groups of people as some of the worst sinners whom they would never want to be associated with. However, these terrible "sinners" were the very people that Jesus compared with the first son. They were people who were initially rebellious against God and did not follow or obey Him, but they listened to the preaching of repentance and changed their lives. Can you think of any tax collectors in the New Testament who decided to follow and obey Jesus? (Matthew and Zaccheus) When Jesus said, "*Assuredly, I say to you that tax collectors and harlots enter the kingdom of God before you,*" those religious leaders probably had their mouths hanging open. What! Those sinners will go to heaven, but we may not?!? Jesus was comparing them to the second son. They would seem like they were very religious. They knew the law and could quote scripture and would tell the people what to do, but they wouldn't obey the Lord by doing His will and His work. They were ones who said, "Lord, Lord," but did not do the will of the Father in heaven.

Read Matthew 21:32. Jesus reveals whose preaching of repentance should have been listened to. Who had come to the Jews in righteousness preaching repentance but was not believed? (John the baptist) The tax collectors and harlots *did* listen to John and believed the truth. No matter what sins were in their past, they had hearts that softened as they heard the word of God. They repented and made changes in their lives as they decided to faithfully follow and serve the Lord. The Jewish religious leaders heard John preach as well but sadly, had hard hearts that would not soften in repentance and obedience.

In this parable, Jesus is teaching us how important it is to obey the Lord. It is great to say we love Him and go to church to worship Him, but we must also be actively serving and obeying Him every day if we are to be truly pleasing to Him.

Review Questions: (Answers are provided in the Answer Key.)

1. How many sons did the man in the parable have?

2. What did the father command his sons to do?

3. When did the work need to be done.

4. How would you describe the way the first son answered his father?

5. How did the first son respond to his father's request?

6. List some examples from the Bible of people who refused to obey God for awhile but then later changed their mind and obeyed Him.

7. What is repentance?

8. How did the second son respond to his father's request?

9. What verse in the New Testament tells us that those who do the will of the Father will enter the kingdom of heaven?

10. In this parable, which son did the will of his father?

11. To whom was Jesus teaching this parable?

12. To which son in the parable did Jesus compare them to?

13. Who did the father in the parable represent?

14. Why would tax collectors and harlots enter the kingdom of heaven before the people Jesus was talking to?

15. Who had come to the Jews preaching repentance but was not believed?

16. What two groups of people did believe the preaching?

 ## "Putting Down Roots": Memory Work

- Memorize Matthew 7:21

- Memorize I Corinthians 15:58

 ## "Add A Leaf": Words To Know

- Righteousness

- Obedience

 ## "Harvest Fun": Games & Activities

- Sword Drill - "*The sword of the Spirit, which is the word of God.*" (Ephesians 6:17) Let's practice using our "swords"! Each person participating needs a Bible. When a reference is called out, everyone tries to find the scripture. The one who finds it first gets to read it aloud, but wait until everyone has turned to it first. The references are from both the Old and New Testament, and all of them have to do with obedience: Luke 6:46; Philippians 2:8; Hebrews 5:8; Genesis 6:22; Ephesians 6:1; Acts 5:29; Esther 2:20; Matthew 8:27; James 3:3; Genesis 28:7; John 14:15; Jeremiah 7:23; Psalm 143:10; Exodus 19:5; II Corinthians 10:5; II John 1:6; Joshua 5:6; Luke 11:28; Romans 5:19; I Samuel 15:22

- Mom Says! - This game is to be played just like Simon Says, only Mom (or the teacher) calls the shots! Listen carefully and only do what Mom says if she starts out by saying, "Mom says.." It is important to obey what we're told by our parents and even more important that we obey what we are told by God. In this lesson's parable, only one son truly obeyed.

"Digging Deeper": Research

- Tax Collectors – Tax collectors were **not** well-liked by the Jews. Who did the tax collectors work for? How much territory did they cover? What were their duties? Why did the people dislike them so much? Can you think of any tax collectors in the New Testament who are mentioned by name?

- "Obedience" concordance search – Look up the word "obedience" in a concordance and try to answer the following questions about this subject: 1) Who all are we to be obedient to? (Both in heaven and on earth) 2) What New Testament scripture tells us that obedience comes from the heart? 3) What New Testament passage of scripture tells us to be obedient to or subject to civil authorities? 4) What does II Thessalonians 1:7-8 tells us will happen to those who do not obey the gospel of Christ? 5) List some examples of Bible characters who demonstrated obedience. Give the passage of scripture and a description of how they obeyed.

"Food For Thought": Puzzles

- What's Missing? - Fill in the missing words from the following scriptures, then choose the correct reference from the box and write it in the parentheses. All quotations are taken from the NKJV. Answers are provided in the Answer Key.

> Matthew 21:29   Matthew 21:32   Matthew 21:28
>
> Matthew 21:30   Matthew 21:31

1. "For _____ came to _____ in the way of _____, and you did not _____ him." (_____)

2. "Which of the _____ did the _____ of his _____?" (_____)

3. "A man had two _____, and he came to the _____ and said, '_____, go, _____ today in my _____.'" (_____)

4. "Then he came to the _____ and said _____. And he _____ and said, 'I go, _____,' but he did not _____." (_____)

5. "He _____ and said, 'I will _____,' but _____ he _____ it and _____." (_____)

- To obey or not to obey? - That is the question! Sometimes obeying can be hard, but it is right and necessary. Look up the following verses, then answer the questions. Answers are provided in the Answer Key.

1. Genesis 6:22 – Who obeyed God? _____ How much of what God commanded him did he obey? _____

2. Haggai 1:7-8, 12 – Who obeyed God? _____

   What had God told them to do? _____

3. Leviticus 10:1 – Who disobeyed God? _____

   How had they disobeyed Him? _____

4. John 8:29 – Who is speaking in this verse? _____ How often did he do things that pleased God? _____

5. I Samuel 15:1-3, 7-9 – What command did God give in verses 1-3? _____

    _____

    Was that command obeyed? _____ Why or why not? _____

    _____

"Fruits Of Our Labor": Crafts

*   Bible Bookmark – Cut white card stock 2 inches wide by 6 inches long, and copy Matthew 7:21 on it: "Not everyone who says to Me, 'Lord, Lord' shall enter the kingdom of heaven, but he who does the will of My Father in heaven." You may want to try calligraphy or cross stitch. Draw a decorative border around it or decorate it any way you choose. When finished, laminate your bookmark. If you'd like, punch a hole near the top and tie a pretty ribbon through it.

*   Illustrate a parable - Illustrate the parable from this lesson. You can continue the same method you have been using or choose a different way to illustrate it.

Lesson 9: Parable of the Laborers

Text: Matthew 20:1-16

"Growing In The Word": Lesson Text & Discussion

Read Matthew 20:1-2. A landowner needed work done in his vineyard so he decided to go out and hire some day laborers. Under the law of Moses, how were such workers to be paid? **Read Deuteronomy 24:15** to find out. (At the end of the day's work) What time of day did the landowner go out and hire laborers? (In the morning) How much did he agree to pay them for a day's work? (A denarius) A denarius was a Roman coin (sometimes called a penny) that was equal to several pennies in our money today (maybe as much as 14 cents). This was a common wage paid to Roman soldiers and other day laborers.

Read Matthew 20:3-4. As the morning progresses, the landowner goes out about the third hour of the day. (There is an interesting research project in this lesson that explores the Jewish day and what time each hour represented.) It is still morning when the landowner goes out into the marketplace, and he sees some men there. How are they described? (Idle) To be idle means to be doing nothing. These men were just standing around, not working, not doing anything important. The landowner offers to hire them as well. What does he agree to pay them? (He tells them he will pay them what is right.) Did the idle men agree to go to work? (Yes)

Read Matthew 20:5. The landowner went out twice more, each time hiring another group of men to go work in his vineyard. At what hours of the day did he do this? (The 6th hour and the 9th hour) Now we are moving into the afternoon time of the day. Will these workers be able to put in a full days' work? (No) Even so, they are willing to go and work as long as there is time.

Read Matthew 20:6-7. This is the fifth and final time the landowner is going to hire a group of workers. He again finds men standing around idle in the marketplace. This time, the landowner asks them why they are just being idle and not working. What answer did they give the landowner? (They said no one had hired them to work.) The landowner tells them to go work in his vineyard. What payment arrangement does he make with them? (He agrees to pay them whatever is right.) The 11th hour of the day would be very late in the afternoon and in fact, be getting close to quitting time, but these men are willing to go and do whatever work they can in the short time they have.

Read Matthew 20:8-12. At last it is quitting time, and the workers start coming in from the vineyard to receive their wages. Who was handing out the money to the workers?

(The steward of the landowner) A steward was a trusted and faithful servant who would handle his master's business transactions for him. You may remember in the Old Testament that Joseph was a steward to his Egyptian master Potiphar. The landowner gave specific instructions to his steward as to the order he was to pay the workers. Who was to be paid first? (Those who were hired last.) Who was to be paid last? (Those who were hired first.) As the workers began receiving their pay, what did those men who were hired at the 11th hour receive for their wages? (A denarius) These men had only worked one hour for the landowner, yet they received a full day's wages. The men who had been hired first thing in the morning saw this. What did they think it meant for them? (They thought they would receive more.) When their turn finally came, how much did the steward pay them for a full day's work? (He paid them each a denarius.) What was the reaction of these men? (They murmured.) They started grumbling and complaining against the landowner. They said it wasn't fair that some men only worked one hour and got paid the same amount as they who had worked and sweated all day long. Was this fair? (Answers may vary.) Let's look at how the landowner handles the complaint of the workers.

Read Matthew 20:13-16. What did the landowner agree to pay the workers he had hired early in the morning? (A denarius) Did the landowner do what he said he would do? (Yes) He also agreed with the other workers throughout the day to pay them "whatever is right." The landowner felt that it was right to pay each one of them a denarius for working in his vineyard. He wanted to give a good reward to each man who had put forth an effort to work for him. Since it was the landowner's money to give, was he allowed to be generous if he wanted to? (Yes!) For the early workers to complain about it made them look envious, selfish, and ungenerous. **Read Philippians 2:14.**

Jesus ends this parable by repeating similar words he spoke before beginning this parable. **Read Matthew 19:30.** He is emphasizing that those who would try to put themselves above others and be first may end up being last while those who are last and don't expect as much may find themselves being first.

So, what does this parable mean for us? The Lord represents the landowner, and He needs workers in His vineyard (the kingdom of God). Some people decide to follow the Lord at a very young age and become a Christian, then serve Him faithfully all of their lives. Some people become a Christian as young adults, or in their middle-aged years, or even when they are quite old and nearing the end of their life. These represent the different hours of the day. Someone who decides to follow the Lord at the 11th hour would be someone who is close to the end of their life and only has a short amount of time to serve God faithfully. Is God still gracious to someone like that, allowing them to enjoy the reward of heaven just as someone who has been a Christian for decades will get to do? (Yes!!) What does grace mean? Grace is when we receive what we do not deserve. None of us can ever "earn" heaven, and God does not owe us salvation. He is a gracious, loving and generous God. While we work in His vineyard, it is not to be "paid" but to willingly serve. Our salvation and reward of a home in heaven is His generous gift of grace given to us. (Ephesians 2:8)

Review Questions: (Answers are provided in the Answer Key.)

1. According to the law of Moses, when were day laborers to be paid?

2. Where did the landowner want work to be done?

3. When did the landowner hire the first group of workers?

4. How many times in all did the landowner hire a group of workers throughout the day?

5. Who was in charge of paying the laborers?

6. What Old Testament steward was mentioned in this lesson?

7. In what order were the workers to be paid?

8. How much was paid to the workers who had been hired at the 11th hour?

9. How long had these men worked in the vineyard?

10. When the men who had been hired first thing in the morning saw this, what did they think it meant for them?

11. What were these men paid?

12. Were these workers satisfied with such payment?

13. What did they say to the landowner about their wages as compared to what the other men were paid?

14. Did the landowner pay them what he had agreed to pay them that morning?

15. Was this landowner a generous man?

16. What does Philippians 2:14 remind us to do?

17. According to Jesus, who will be first and who will be last?

18. Does the age you become a Christian and years of service you have in the kingdom of God determine how much of a reward you will receive from God?

19. What is grace?

20. What is God's gift of grace to us?

 ## "Putting Down Roots": Memory Work

- Memorize Matthew 20:16

- Memorize Philippians 2:14

 ## "Add A Leaf": Words To Know

- Idle

- Steward

- Grace

 ## "Harvest Fun": Games & Activities

- You First! - This is a brainstorming activity, so put your thinking caps on! Discuss this parable and why it was so difficult for the workers who started early to be charitable to those who started working later. What might have helped them change their attitudes toward their fellow workers? Sometimes, it can be difficult to put others and their needs first before ourselves, can't it? Think of some situations where we can take an opportunity to put someone else first, be it easy or hard, then work on putting it into practice every opportunity you get.

- Act it Out! - This would be another good parable to act out. The characters would be: the landowner and the workers. You could create a good scene with the workers who felt they were treated unfairly. (You could portray them really whining and complaining to the master.) Dress in costume if you'd like, but pay attention to the detail of this lesson. Remember to emphasize the attitude of the landowner. Video this scene if you'd like or perform it in front of friends and family, then discuss the lessons we can all learn from this parable of Jesus.

 ## "Digging Deeper": Research

- Vineyards – Grapes were an "in demand" crop in Bible times, due to the fact that much of what was drunk by people was the "fruit of the vine" which was grape juice or wine, and also, the fruit itself was eaten or dried into raisins. Therefore, it was important to have healthy vineyards to grow the grapes and to produce a good crop. Do some research into ancient vineyards and try to answer the following questions: Where were vineyards usually planted and why? What surrounded them? What two things were usually built at the site of the vineyard? How many verses can you find in the Bible that mention a vineyard?

- Jewish day – Our 24 hour day begins at 12:00 a.m. (midnight), but the Jewish day was oriented differently. Find out what time the Jewish day started and how it was divided, then try to figure out what time it would be for the different hours of the day mentioned in this parable: 3rd hour - _____, 6th hour - _____, 9th hour - _____, 11th hour - _____ (Answers are provided in the Answer Key.)

 ## "Food For Thought": Puzzles

- True or False? - Read each statement, then decide if it is true or false. Write the answer on the line. Answers are provided in the Answer Key.

_____ 1. "But when the first came, they supposed that they would receive more."

_____ 2. "And when those came who were hired about the tenth hour, they each received a denarius."

_____ 3. "For the kingdom of heaven is like a landowner who went out early in the morning to hire laborers for his fields."

_____ 4. "And he went out about the third hour and saw others standing idle in the marketplace."

_____ 5. "And when they had received it, they praised the landowner."

_____ 6. "But he answered one of them and said, 'Friend, I am doing you no wrong.'"

_____ 7. "So the last will be first, and the first last."

_____ 8. "Again he went out about the sixth and the ninth hour, and did likewise."

_____ 9. "For many are called, and many are chosen."

_____ 10. "He said to them, 'You also go into the vineyard, and whatever is right you will receive.'"

- What Happened Next? - Read the following statements, then answer with what immediately followed. Answers are provided in the Answer Key.

1. A landowner went out early in the morning to hire laborers to work in his vineyard.

_____

2. The landowner went into the marketplace about the 3rd hour of the day and saw some standing idle. _____

_____

3. He went out about the 11th hour of the day and found others standing idle.

   _____

4. The workers who were hired first in the morning received their wages.

   _____

5. The landowner told the workers who had been hired first that they had received the wages that had been agreed upon. _____

   _____

 ## "Fruits Of Our Labor": Crafts

- Clock craft – In this parable, a lot of people were very concerned about time! Let's make a decoupage clock to remind us that the Lord's timing is always right. For this craft you will need the following: A rectangular wood plaque, a set of clock works (including hands), adhesive numbers 1-12 for the clock face, paint color of your choice, scrapbook paper of your choice, glue and a sponge brush. First, you will need a wooden plaque with a pre-drilled hole for the clock hands, or have an adult drill a 3/8" hole in the position where you want the clock hands to go. Next, paint your wooden plaque in the color of your choice and let it dry completely. Next, trim your scrapbook paper to a size that will fit the plaque, but still let a border of color show all around the edges. Use the sponge brush to glue the paper onto the plaque. While glue is still damp, gently press the paper where the hole is with the tip of a pencil or pen to open it up. Once the paper is dry, write "Wait on the Lord" -Isaiah 40:31 somewhere on the paper below where the numbers will be placed. Place the self-adhesive numbers around the hole at a distance far enough way from the hole so the clock hands will not touch them. The easiest way would be to place the 12, the 6, then the 3 and the 9 followed by the other numbers in between. Insert the clockworks shaft through the hole in the back towards the front. Place the clock hands on the shaft.

- Illustrate a parable – Illustrate the parable from this lesson. You can continue the same method you have been using or choose a different way to illustrate it.

Lesson 10: Parables of the Ambitious Guests & the Great Feast

Text: Luke 14:7-14, 15-24

"Growing In The Word": Lesson Text & Discussion

Read Luke 14:7. We see from this verse that Jesus is going to tell a parable to those who were invited...invited to what and by whom? Back in verse 1 of this chapter, we read that one of the rulers of the Pharisees was hosting Jesus at his house, but we also see from verse 7 that there were many other invited guests as well. As Jesus looked around, he noticed something about these invited guests. What was it? (They were choosing the best places for themselves.) Usually when someone invites you to their home for a meal, they will either tell you where they would like you to sit, or they will invite you to sit wherever you'd like. These guests weren't waiting for their host to give them any such instructions, they were simply taking the best seats because they wanted them. Jesus used this "teachable moment" to tell them a parable.

Read Luke 14:8-10. Jesus begins by giving them a lesson in etiquette. Do you know what etiquette means? It is the practice of good manners and behavior. Jesus reminds the guests that it is not good manners to seat yourselves in the best places when you are invited to a feast such as a wedding feast. What does he say might happen in that situation? (The host who invited them might have to tell them to a move to a different seat that is not as good and then they would be embarrassed.) In Bible times, a feast would usually involve a table with the host seated at the head. Then, he would have places of honor to his right and left but as you moved farther away from the host, those seats were for people of younger age or lesser in rank. The seats of honor were generally reserved for those who were older and those who held an important rank or title or who were a specially invited guest of honor. For example, someone might invite several guests for a dinner, among which would be his grandfather, a ruler of the Pharisees, an elderly Jewish rabbi, and other friends and tradesmen from the town. The host would seat his grandfather, the ruler, and the rabbi in seats of honor close to him, then seat the remaining friends and tradesmen in order of their age and/or their position (wealth, status in society, etc.) So what Jesus is saying is don't rudely take the best seats for yourselves and then face humiliation when someone older or more important arrives and the host has to tell you to move! Instead, what does Jesus advise they should do? (Seat themselves in the lowest places and let the host come to them and move them to a better seat.) This would be practicing good etiquette as well as showing humility. What does it mean to be humble? To be humble means to think more highly of others than yourself and to put others first. If one is humble, he will not take the best seat for himself but will thoughtfully leave it for someone else. Then you might be pleasantly surprised when you are moved to a position of honor because of your humble attitude.

Read Luke 14:11. What does Jesus say will happen to those who want to exalt themselves? (They will be brought low.) To exalt means to lift high or raise to a rank of high position or power. Those who exalt themselves will often find themselves (sometimes in an embarrassing or humiliating way) being lowered by others. On the other hand, what will happen to those who have a humble heart? (They will be exalted.) **Read Philippians 2:3.** We shouldn't want to do things because it will promote or exalt ourselves in some way. That is selfishness. Instead, we should work on having a humble attitude that puts the needs and interests of others before ourselves.

Read Luke 14:12-14. Now Jesus turns his attention from the guests at the feast to the host who invited him. He has some instructions for him as well. Whom does he say should *not* invite to dinner? (He should not invite his friends, brothers, relatives, or rich neighbors.) Those are some tough instructions, aren't they? We like to have dinners and parties with our friends and family. It's not that it is wrong to do that, but Jesus is making a point to this particular ruler of the Pharisees. He had been guilty of *only* inviting those kinds of people, so others who should have been invited and shown hospitality were being neglected. Whom does Jesus say he *should* invite? (The poor, the maimed, the lame and the blind) Apparently, this Pharisee was rich and had a lot of rich friends and family. All of those people could take turns inviting each other to their houses. They were all able to repay the generous hospitality of an expensive meal with a feast of their own. But there were those who didn't often get invited to a nice dinner or anywhere else for that matter. Many of the poor and handicapped people of Jesus' day were neglected. The rich usually didn't bother with them because there was nothing the poor could do for them in return. They certainly couldn't afford to repay a rich host by hosting their own lavish banquet and inviting the rich. But Jesus again stresses the quality of humility – think of others needs and interests before your own. Jesus wants this ruler of the Pharisees to be compassionate and invite people who need a good meal but can do nothing to repay the kindness of being invited to such a feast. Even though the poor guests cannot repay such a host, he will still be repaid. When does Jesus say that will happen? (At the resurrection) God sees all and knows all and nothing will go unrewarded that He wants to reward.

Read Luke 14:15. One of the guests had been carefully listening to all that Jesus has been saying. He bursts out about how wonderful it will be to eat bread in the kingdom of God. Unfortunately, Jesus knows that far too many don't care about God's kingdom or appreciate all of the blessings in it. This leads him to tell another parable to the guests at this feast.

Read Luke 14:16-20. Jesus tells the story of a man who was giving a great banquet and had invited lots of guests. When everything was ready, he sent out a servant to inform all of those who had been invited that it was time to come to the feast. This was a custom in ancient times, to extend a second invitation to those who had been invited. Did the guests start flocking to this man's house? (No) They began to give excuses as to why they could not come. What were the excuses given? (1-One had bought land and had to go see it. 2-One had bought oxen and had to go test them out. 3-One had just gotten married.) This is very rude! These guests knew the man was preparing to serve a banquet and had gotten all of the food and drinks ready, then at the last minute they say have more important things to do and can't come. If you were the host, how would this make you feel? (Answers will vary.)

Read Luke 14:21-22. How did the master of the feast react to the news his servant brought back to him about the guests and their excuses? (He was angry.) Even though he was angry at the disrespectful guests, it didn't make him pack up all the food and call it a day. What did he tell his servant to do? (He told his servant to go out into the streets of the city and bring in the poor, the crippled and the blind.) After the servant followed his master's instructions, what was the problem then? (There was still room for more at the feast.)

Read Luke 14:23-24. What did the master tell the servant to do this time? (He told him to go out into the highways and bushes and find anyone he could to bring to the feast.) The master had prepared a wonderful banquet, and he wanted his house to be completely full of guests. The dinner would begin once his servant was successful in filling all of the places. Who would *not* be there? (None of those who had originally been invited and offered excuses would be at the feast.)

Both of these parables emphasize some similar things. They both show the need for compassion in reaching out to the poor and those who need help. They also show the need to have a humble heart that considers the needs of others before one's self. In the second parable, Jesus shows us that entering the kingdom of God is like coming to a wonderful banquet. It is a place of happiness and joy with good things abounding. Although the Lord invites all to come, not everyone will enter. Some will make excuses or just not have any interest in what the Lord has to offer. Isn't that sad? The good news is that the gospel is for all. God's invitation to come is available to us. He wants His house to be full!

Review Questions: (Answers are provided in the Answer Key.)

1. Who had invited people to dine at his house?

2. What did Jesus notice about the guests who had arrived?

3. If you were practicing good manners, where would you sit at a feast you were invited to?

4. When someone is humble, whose interests does he consider?

5. What does Jesus say will happen to those who exalt themselves?

6. What does Jesus say will happen to those who humble themselves?

7. Whom does Jesus tell the host not to invite to dinner?

8. Whom does Jesus tell the host he should invite to dinner?

9. In the second parable, the Great Supper, what happened to the first set of guests who had been invited?

10. What was the reaction of the master to all of this?

11. What did the master command his servant to do?

12. Did this fill all of the seats at the banquet?

13. What was the next command the master gave his servant?

14. Who would *not* be at the great banquet?

15. In the second parable, who does the master represent and what does the invitation to the banquet represent?

 "Putting Down Roots": Memory Work

- Memorize Luke 14:11

- Memorize Philippians 2:3

"Add A Leaf": Words To Know

- Etiquette

- Humble

- Exalt

"Harvest Fun": Games & Activities

- Scripture race - This game is for two players or two teams. Write out Luke 14:10 on two different-colored index cards, one word per card, or phrase per card. Assign a color to each player or team. Let someone who is not playing mix up and hide all of the cards throughout the house or a large room. When "Go!" is called, let the players race around the room to find all of the cards in their color and assemble their scripture. The first player or team to collect all of their cards and correctly put their scripture in order wins. (Bibles may be used to assist when ordering the cards.)

- Prepare a feast! - Plan a meal at your house and plan on who you'd like to invite. You could do an indoor picnic, a tea party, a dessert buffet, a taco fest, pizza party, or fancy dinner. You can go as simple or elaborate as you want with this activity; it's up to you! The most important thing to plan is the guest list. Who can you invite that might really appreciate the invitation? A widow from church? Some kids from church or the neighborhood whose family may be struggling financially? A kid that you know who is lonely and needs a friend? Remember that Jesus taught that one would be blessed who invited guests who could never repay the hospitality. (Luke 14:13-14)

"Digging Deeper": Research

- Wedding Feasts - How were weddings celebrated in Bible times? In some ways, they were similar to weddings today and in other ways, they were very different! See what you can learn about weddings in Bible times and in particular, learn what you can about the wedding feast.

- Humility word study – Find the word "humility" in a concordance and answer the following questions: 1) Which New Testament scripture tells us to wear humility like clothing? 2) What two Old Testament verses say "before honor is humility"? 3) What New Testament book contains two verses about false humility in the same chapter?

"Food For Thought": Puzzles

- Which Parable? - We studied two parables of Jesus in this lesson, the parable of the ambitious guests and the parable of the great feast. Read the following clues, then write the correct answer on the line. Answers will be used more than once, and some clues have more than one answer. Answers are provided in the Answer Key.

1. In which parable did invited guests make excuses? _____

2. Which parable contained advice about who to invite to your dinner party? _____

_____

3. Which parable had a host or master of the feast? _____

4. In which parable did the host have to move a guest to another place to sit? _____

_____

5. Which parable involved a meal with invited guests? _____

6. In which parable did the master of the feast become angry? _____

   _____

7. In which parable did invited guests refuse to come to dinner? _____

   _____

8. Which parable teaches us about humility? _____

9. Which parable tells us that we will be blessed when we extend hospitality to those who cannot repay it? _____

10. In which parable were poor people invited to dinner? _____

- Search the Scriptures - Look up the following scriptures to see if they are printed correctly. If something is not right, cross it out and make the correction. Quotations are taken from the NKJV. Answers are provided in the Answer Key.

1. "But when you give a feast, invite the rich, the maimed, the lame, the blind." (Luke 14:13)

2. "But they all with one accord began to make excuses. The third one said to him, 'I have bought a yoke of oxen, and I must go and see them. I ask you to have me another time." (Luke 14:18)

3. "When you are invited to a wedding ceremony, do not sit down in the front row, lest one more important than you be invited by him." (Luke 14:8)

4. "Then the master said to the mistress, 'Go out into the alleys and hedges, and beg them to come in, that my castle may be filled.'" (Luke 14:23)

5. "So He told a story to those who were there, when He noted how they chose the quietest places." (Luke 14:7)

"Fruits Of Our Labor": Crafts

- Design an invitation - In both of these parables, people were invited to a dinner. These invitations were most likely made by sending a servant or helper to ask the guests to come. We can still invite people the same way today – just by asking them, but have you ever received a written invitation to a party or some other event? Written invitations can be very fun or fancy, but they are also helpful because all of the information about the event you've been invited to is contained in it. For this craft, you will be designing an invitation to invite people to church. There are many ways you can decorate an invitation – using scrapbook papers or colored card stock, trimming edges with special scissors or using cutouts from Cricut machines, stickers, ribbons, and on and on! The most important thing about this invitation is the information to include. You want the people you're inviting to know the times of services and the location of the church. Maybe you could also include your favorite Bible verse or a picture of the church building. Be creative and make as many of these as you would like, then think about who you can invite. What about the cashier at the grocery store? The librarian? A waiter or waitress at a restaurant? Your neighbor or friend?

- Illustrate a parable - Illustrate a parable from this lesson, or do both if you'd like. You can continue the same method you have been using or choose a different way to illustrate it.

Lesson 11: Parable of the Sheep & Goats

Text: Matthew 25:31-46

"Growing In The Word": Lesson Text & Discussion

Read Matthew 25:31-33. Based on the description of the "Son of Man" in this passage, who do you think he is? He will come in glory with angels and sit on His throne in glory. Then all people will be gathered before him. This Son of Man is Jesus Christ, and these verses are talking about the second coming of Jesus and the day when all will be judged by him. On that day, he will divide the righteous from the wicked. How is that described in these verses? (It is described as a shepherd dividing the sheep from the goats.) Where will the sheep be located and where will the goats be located? (The sheep will be at his right hand and the goats will be at his left.) To be placed at the right hand of someone was considered a special place of favor and honor. So if the sheep are placed at the right hand of the Son of Man, does that mean they represent the righteous or the wicked? (The righteous)

Read Matthew 25:34. Jesus isn't called the Son of Man in this verse but something else. How is he referred to? (He is called the King.) He has a special message for the sheep he has placed at his right hand. What does he say to them? ("*Come, you blessed of My Father, inherit the kingdom prepared for you from the foundation of the world.*") Do you know what an inheritance is? An inheritance is to receive something from someone after they die. Children are usually heirs of their parents. When the parents die, the children receive an inheritance from them such as their house, land, money or possessions. **Read Romans 8:16-17.** According to these verses, whose children are we? (God's) Since Jesus is the Son of God, he is an heir, but since we also are called children of God, we get to be heirs with Jesus! This inheritance the sheep will receive has been prepared and waiting for them for a long time. When did God plan and prepare this inheritance for His children? (Before the world and people were ever created)

Read Matthew 25:35-36. The King explains to the sheep why they are receiving a wonderful inheritance from Him. There were many acts of service and compassion which the sheep had been busy doing in their lifetimes. The King told them He was pleased with them for feeding Him when He was hungry, giving Him something to drink when He was thirsty, giving Him a place to stay when He needed shelter, giving Him clothes when He didn't have any, and visiting Him when He was sick and in prison. That is quite a list! It sounds like these sheep were very faithful servants to their King, and they were, but not quite in the way they had thought about it. They listen to the King praising them, but they are going to have a few questions about all of this.

Read Matthew 25:37-39. The sheep are now called "the righteous" in these verses. They ask the Lord their King several questions, but they all really boil down to just one question. What was it? (When did we ever do these things for you personally?) This shows their humility. They had spent their lives looking out for the needs and interests of others, and every time they saw a need they could fill, they willingly filled it. They weren't thinking about impressing their King by their good deeds. They weren't keeping track of their good works in a book, hoping to do enough to get a prize. They weren't helping others to show off how good they were. They simply lived lives that the righteous live – they would do what was right. And that was enough for them. They didn't feel that they deserved such high praise from their King.

Read Matthew 25:40. The King acknowledges that they may have not done these good deeds to Him personally, but whenever they helped anyone who was in need, it was the same as if they were doing it for the King himself. The King refers to them helping "the least." Who do you think He means? (Answers will vary.) The least could mean those who were very poor, or any who were neglected by society and had no one to help them. It was always right for the righteous to help anyone they could, but it was especially important to help those who were completely helpless. **Read Colossians 3:23-24.** Everything we do for others should be done just as if we were doing it to the Lord himself because according to these verses, who are we really serving? (The Lord Jesus Christ)

Read Matthew 25:41-43. Now the King turns His attention from the righteous sheep on His right to the goats on His left. What is the opposite of being righteous? (Being wicked) The goats have been separated from the sheep because they were wicked in the sight of the King. Just as the righteous were rewarded, the wicked will be punished. Where does the King tell the wicked they will go? (They will go into everlasting fire.) This is a place of punishment that was prepared for the devil and his angels. It is a separation from Jesus Christ the King. This should make us determined to be sheep and not goats! While the righteous sheep had spent their lives serving the Lord by serving others, the goats had done just the opposite. The Lord tells them that they had had many opportunities for doing good but neglected to do them. **Read James 4:17.** It was not enough for the goats to just avoid sin. There were opportunities all around them to serve, but they did nothing.

Read Matthew 25:44-45. The wicked goats try to make excuses. Does it work with the King? (No) They protest that they never saw the King in need of anything so they weren't to blame for failing to serve. They claim there was no opportunity to minister to Him directly. To minister to someone means to wait upon them, to tend to them, to serve them. If they had humble, loving hearts that truly wanted to serve the King, they would have been willingly serving others every chance they had, but they didn't. It wasn't that they never saw anyone who needed help. It was that they had hard, selfish hearts that didn't care about helping anyone but themselves. The King points out to them that every time they refused to help the least, they were refusing to serve the King. There was no excuse. Period.

Read Matthew 25:46. Jesus concludes the parable by again talking about the sheep and the goats being separated. Where will the wicked goats go? (They will go into everlasting punishment.) Where will the righteous sheep go? (They will go into eternal life.) Eternal means forever, never-ending. What a wonderful thought that one day we can be with our King forever and ever!

This parable shows us how important it is to be aware of others and have a heart for service. There are needs all around us if we will just open our eyes and hearts to them. We can't be too busy, too tired, or certainly not too uncaring. We should look at every opportunity to serve others as a chance to serve the Lord our King and be thankful for it.

Review Questions: (Answers are provided in the Answer Key.)

1. Who is the "Son of Man?"

2. On the day of judgment, where will he set the sheep and where will he set the goats?

3. Which position was a place of favor and honor?

4. Who calls the sheep, *"you blessed of My Father"*?

5. What inheritance will the sheep receive?

6. When was this inheritance prepared by God?

7. Why was the King pleased with the sheep?

8. Why did the righteous question what the King praised them for?

9. How did the King answer them?

10. According to Colossians 3:23-24, who are we ultimately serving as we go about serving others?

11. What is the opposite of righteousness?

12. Where were the goats to be sent as punishment?

13. Who else would be there?

14. What excuse did the wicked offer for not serving the Lord?

15. Was this excuse acceptable to the King?

16. What does James 4:17 tell us about failing to do good when we know we should do it?

17. Where does Jesus say the righteous will go?

 "Putting Down Roots": Memory Work

• Memorize Matthew 25:34-36

• Memorize Colossians 3:23-24

• Memorize James 4:17

 "Add A Leaf": Words To Know

• Inheritance

• Minister

• Eternal

 "Harvest Fun": Games & Activities

• Sheep or Goat? - For this game, each player needs two index cards. On one card write "sheep", on the other card write "goats." In this parable, the sheep represented the righteous while the goats represented those who did not obey or please God. As each clue is read aloud, players will hold up the correct answer card. You may keep score individually, play as teams, or just play for review and fun!

1. The King set us on his right hand. (Sheep)

2. The King told us to depart from him. (Goats)

3. We saw people who needed help. (Both)

4. We were sent into everlasting punishment. (Goats)

5. We were under the authority of the King. (Both)

6. We were invited to inherit the kingdom prepared for us from the foundation of the world. (Sheep)

7. The King placed us at his left hand. (Goats)

8. We were gathered together before the king. (Both)

9. We helped anyone who needed it. (Sheep)

10. We asked the King, "Lord, when did we see You hungry and feed You, or thirsty and give You drink? When did we see You a stranger and take You in, or naked and clothe You", or when did we see You sick, or in prison, and come to You?" (Both)

11. The King answered us, "Assuredly, I say to you, inasmuch as you did it to one of the least of these My brethren, you did it to Me." (Sheep)

12. The King told us that we had fed him, given him drink, took him in, clothed him, and visited him. (Sheep)

13. The King told us that because we had not helped even the least, we had not helped him. (Goats)

14. We were told to depart from the King. (Goats)

15. We had an obligation to help everyone we could whether we realized it was as if we were serving the Lord or not. (Both)

- "Goat, Goat, Sheep!" Game – This game is played like "Duck, Duck, Goose." Players will sit in a circle with a chair representing the throne of the king placed in the center. One player will walk slowly around the circle, touching each player's head as he walks and saying, "Goat, goat, goat..." until he decides to label a player as a sheep. Whoever was tagged sheep must jump up and chase the tagger around the circle trying to tag him back. The tagger must try to outrun him and make it safely into the circle, sitting down next to the throne. Then the "sheep" gets to be the tagger, or if the first tagger didn't make it to safety, he will continue around the circle again. After playing the game, discuss what qualities the King saw in his sheep, how we can imitate those in our own lives, and why we should all want to be "sheep".

- "I Just Want to Be a Sheep!" - If you know this song...you know you have to sing it with this lesson! If you don't know it, there are links online (ask for permission and/or supervision) that have all of the lyrics and hand motions. But be warned – once you learn this fun song, it is easy to get it stuck in your head!

 ## "Digging Deeper": Research

- Right hand – Have you ever heard the expression "right hand man"? Typically, the right hand symbolizes power and strength. There are many instances of "the right hand" occurring in scripture with this meaning, but there are also other meanings or representations. Read the following verses and try to answer the questions. Genesis 35:18 – Which son of Jacob had a name which meant "son of my right hand"? Genesis 48:14-16 – What was the right hand used for in this passage? Exodus 15:6, 12 – What did the right hand of the Lord do or represent? Psalm 60:5; Isaiah 41:10 – What was the right hand of the Lord able to do? Psalm 45:9; Psalm 110:1; Matthew 26:64 – What does the right hand represent in these verses?

- Prisons – Being a prisoner in Bible times was quite different from what it is like today. In the parable from this lesson, one of the things that the righteous did to those less fortunate than them was to visit them in prison. This would most likely not have been just a visit to stop by and say "hi", but probably would have been a way of helping the prisoners in their time of distress. Research what prison life would have been like. Where were prisoners kept? How were they confined? Besides breaking a law (such as stealing), what else could a person be thrown in prison for? Were conditions clean or harsh? Would a prisoner be fed by his captors or would he have to rely on others from the outside to bring him food?

"Food For Thought": Puzzles

- Matching – Match the word or phrase on the left with its description or meaning on the right. Answers are provided in the Answer Key.

_____ 1. The righteous   a. Needed visiting

_____ 2. Holy angels   b. Those on the left hand

_____ 3. Sheep   c. Needed a place to stay

_____ 4. Son of Man   d. Everlasting fire has been prepared for him

_____ 5. Shepherd   e. Will go into eternal life

_____ 6. Goats   f. Will come with the Son of Man

_____ 7. King   g. Those on the right hand

_____ 8. Stranger   h. Divides the sheep from the goats

_____ 9. Prisoner   i. Will come in glory

_____ 10. The devil   j. Gives an inheritance to those on his right

• Crossword Puzzle – If an answer contains more than one word, the space is included. Answers are provided in the Answer Key.

Across

1 These will accompany the Son of Man when he comes in his glory.

4 These are those whom the righteous did things for.

7 This is what the righteous will enter into.

8 Those on the left were told to do this.

9 He divides the sheep from the goats.

11 "Inasmuch as you did it to one of the least of these My _____, you did it to Me."

13 These were placed on the right hand of the King.

14 These were placed on the left hand of the King.

15 The _____ asked, "Lord, when did we see you hungry?"

Down

2 This was prepared for the devil and his angels.

3 The King prepared a kingdom before the foundation of the _____.

5 The righteous would inherit this from the King.

6 He needed a place to stay.

10 This is what the Son of Man will be seated on.

12 All of these will be gathered before the Son of Man.

"Fruits Of Our Labor": Crafts

- Diorama - A diorama is simply a scene in miniature and the possibilities are endless as to how to make one! For this diorama, you will create a scene of a shepherd dividing the sheep from the goats to serve as a visual aid to tell the parable from this lesson to someone. Start with a sturdy base such as a piece of wood, or you can turn a shoebox on its side and use the inside of it. Use paints, construction paper, craft foam, or whatever else you'd like to make the sky and other scenery such as trees, grass or bushes. You can also find diorama scenery items at craft stores as well as miniature animals, people and trees. You could use a strip of sandpaper for a road or glue small pebbles for rocks. There are several resources including books, websites and Pinterest that have many great ideas and tips for making some really cool dioramas. Use your imagination and have fun!

- Illustrate a parable - Illustrate the parable from this lesson. You can continue the same method you have been using or choose a different way to illustrate it.

Lesson 12: Parable of the Pharisee & Tax Collector

Text: Luke 18:9-14

"Growing In The Word": Lesson Text & Discussion

Read Luke 18:9. Jesus is going to tell a parable about two men, a Pharisee and a tax collector (or publican), and he has a specific audience he wants to tell it to. To whom did Jesus speak this parable? (He told it to ones who thought they were very righteous while despising others.) This may sound very familiar. Remember the parable of the two sons we studied about in Lesson 8? In that parable, the Jewish religious leaders thought they were going to heaven because they were so righteous and couldn't believe their ears when Jesus talked about tax collectors and harlots making it to heaven before them. The Pharisees were some of those Jewish religious leaders. They were known to be experts in knowing the law of Moses, and many of them made quite of show of being very religious. However, they were very full of pride and hypocrisy. Do you know what it means to be a hypocrite? A hypocrite is a person who doesn't practice what he preaches. Pharisees enjoyed telling the Jews what they needed to do to obey God, yet they wouldn't practice it themselves. Jesus had a lot to say to them about their self-righteousness and it wasn't complimentary! He spends almost the entire chapter of Matthew 23 condemning them. **Read Matthew 23:3.** Jesus told the Jews that they needed to listen to the teachings of their religious teachers because they taught the truth, but they shouldn't follow their example. Why? (They didn't practice what they preached!)

Read Luke 18:10. Where did the two men go to pray? (To the temple) We just learned about what kind of men the Pharisees were. Do you remember what they and other Jews thought about tax collectors? (They thought tax collectors were liars, cheats, and thieves.) So these are the two men who have "gone to church" to pray. One considered himself very righteous and would have looked down his nose at this "sinner" tax collector who dared to pray near him.

Read Luke 18:11-12. Here we read the prayer of the Pharisee. How would you describe it? (Answers will vary.) Would you say that this is a prayer that God would be pleased with? Is it humble, thankful to God, thoughtful of the needs of others, sorrowful over sin? No! It is very boastful and prideful. This Pharisee is reminding God how good he (the Pharisee) is and how lucky God is to have such a "faithful" follower. He lists all of the good things he has done and all of the bad things he has avoided. What were the good things he listed? (He fasted twice a week and gave tithes of everything he had.) Fasting is when you refrain from something (usually food) for a certain period of time to focus on spiritual things or grieving. The Pharisees loved to walk around in front of everyone with a sad face to let everyone know that they were fasting and suffering for the Lord. Then they would be praised for being so devoted to God, but that was exactly what they were looking for – the praise of men. **Read Matthew 6:16.** This is another example of how they were hypocrites. They taught others to fast and were appearing to fast themselves but not really doing it or were not doing it for the right reasons. Tithing is giving a tenth of something you have to someone else, usually God. What did the Pharisee say he gave tithes of? (Everything he owned) This would mean he was giving a tenth of his flocks or herds, money, and food even down to the spices he had in his kitchen. Faithful Jews practiced tithing but actually gave much more than ten percent. (You will learn more about tithing in one of the research projects for this lesson.) The Pharisee is bragging about all of the good things he has done to follow the law of Moses. Instead, he should have remembered some of the wise words of King Solomon from the book of Proverbs. **Read Proverbs 27:2.** As to the bad things he has avoided, he thanks God that he is not like other terrible sinners such as...who? (Extortioners, unjust, adulterers, tax collectors) An extortioner is someone who takes property or money away from someone by force or violence, or who takes advantage of someone such as the poor. Someone who is unjust lies, cheats, and is dishonest. An adulterer is someone who is not faithful in their marriage, and we have already studied about tax collectors and some of the things they would do. Remember who else is in the temple praying at the same time as the Pharisee? (A tax collector) You can almost see the look on the Pharisee's face as he glances toward him while thanking God that he is not like other terrible men, such as this tax collector. The huge mistake this Pharisee is making is failing to see that he is a sinner too. The Pharisee trusts in his own good works and thinks that God "owes him" salvation. Now let's look at the tax collector's prayer.

Read Luke 18:13. This prayer is quite different from the prayer of the Pharisee! First of all, what was the attitude and prayer posture of the tax collector? In other words, what was he doing as he prayed? (He looked down and beat his chest as he prayed.) The tax collector shows a very different attitude than the Pharisee. While the Pharisee was proud and arrogant, this man is very humble before God. He looks down and not up to the heavens. He beats on his chest with his fist as a sign of deep grief which was a common practice at that time. Why do think he feels such deep sorrow? (Answers may vary.) He is sorrowful over his sin. In the sermon on the mount, Jesus said, *"Blessed are those who mourn, for they shall be comforted."* (Matthew 5:4) Jesus was talking about those who mourn over their sin and feel sorrow over the ways they have hurt God. They will be comforted and blessed through forgiveness. What did the tax collector pray to God? (*"God be merciful to me a sinner!"*) That is quite a short prayer but one full of meaning. The tax collector cried out to God for mercy.

He wanted to receive that blessing of forgiveness and the comfort that Jesus promised it would bring.

Read Luke 18:14. The short parable is finished and Jesus explains whose prayer was acceptable, whose was not, and why. The tax collector went home justified which means his prayer was pleasing and acceptable to God. Was the Pharisee able to go home justified as well? (No!) Jesus explains that anyone who lifts themselves up with pride and arrogance, like the Pharisee, will be brought low while anyone who humbles or lowers himself, such as the tax collector, will be exalted or lifted up. **James 4:10** tells us, *"Humble yourselves in the sight of the Lord, and He will lift you up."*

This short parable has a lot to teach us about how to pray, and about pride and humility.

<u>Review Questions</u>: (Answers are provided in the Answer Key.)

1. To whom did Jesus tell this parable?

2. What chapter in Matthew is full of Jesus' condemnation of the Pharisees?

3. What was the Pharisees' problem?

4. Where did the Pharisee and tax collector go to pray?

5. Describe the Pharisee's prayer.

6. What four groups of people did the Pharisee mention in his prayer that he was thankful he was "not like"?

7. What good works did the Pharisee list in his prayer?

8. What was the tax collector doing as he prayed?

9. Quote the tax collector's prayer.

10. Which prayer did Jesus say was acceptable?

11. What happens to someone who lifts themselves up in pride?

12. What happens to those who humble themselves?

13. What New Testament scripture tells us what will happen if we humble ourselves in the sight of the Lord?

"Putting Down Roots": Memory Work

- Memorize Luke 18:14

- James 4:10

- Proverbs 27:2

"Add A Leaf": Words To Know

- Hypocrite

- Extortioner

- Tithes

- Justified

"Harvest Fun": Games & Activities

- Acceptable Prayer – In the parable studied in this lesson, we saw two examples of prayer: the right way and the wrong way! God delights in humble obedient hearts and finds the prayers that come from such acceptable to Him. Proud hearts and hearts that are full of sin cannot offer acceptable prayers to God. For this game, you will need two teams consisting of one player each or multiple players. Each team needs to have two labels written and hung up on a whiteboard, magnetic board or something that multiple pieces of paper can be stuck on. For the two labels, one should read "Acceptable Prayer" and the other "Unacceptable Prayer." A scorekeeper (or referee if score is not being kept) will make two copies each of the following references on separate slips of paper and place one set each in two envelopes: Proverbs 28:9; I John 5:14; Exodus 34:8-9; Psalm 66:18; James 4:3; Philippians 4:6-7; I Thessalonians 5:16-18; James 1:6b-8; Matthew 6:7; Proverbs 21:13. To begin, each team needs a Bible and an envelope containing the scripture slips of paper. When "Go" is called, let each team open their envelopes, then begin looking up and reading each scripture. As they decide which column the verse belongs to, they will race up to the board and place that scripture in the correct column, "Acceptable Prayer" or "Unacceptable Prayer." The game is finished when one team places their last slip of paper on the board, or play can continue until the other team is finished, at which time, the referee will count up the correct number of answers for each team. If time permits, discuss some of these scriptures. Answers are provided in the Answer Key.

- Obstacle Course – Your goal is to put all obstacles to acceptable prayer behind you and "go down to your house justified." To begin, set up an obstacle course any way you would like in a back yard or very large indoor room. You can use things like pool noodle arches to crawl under, tires to jump in and out of, safety cones to zig zag around, rolling a hula hoop around wooden stakes, etc. There are many online resources for obstacles courses with some great ideas. Once the course is completely set up, place labels on the obstacles that can hinder our prayers, one per obstacle: Pride, arrogance, sin, boasting, conceit, selfishness, hatred, unrepentant, hard-hearted, etc. (Refer to the lesson for more ideas or brainstorm.) At the finish line, place a large poster board with a drawing of your house on it. The object of this activity is to successfully navigate the obstacle course in the quickest amount of time, leaving all obstacles to acceptable prayer behind you and arriving at your house justified just as the tax collector did in the parable.

"Digging Deeper": Research

- Tithing – In the parable studied in this lesson, the Pharisee boasted that he paid tithes of all that he possessed. Under the Law of Moses, how much were faithful Jews to tithe? What possessions were they to pay tithes of? There were three categories which these tithes were divided into. What were they? Read the following scriptures to help you answer these questions: Leviticus 27:30-32; Numbers 18:21-24; Deuteronomy 14:22-27, 26:12-13. A Bible dictionary may also be helpful with this research topic. Bonus questions: What man paid tithes to another man in the Old Testament? Who were the tithes paid to?

- Humble/Arrogant – There is no shortage in the Bible of examples of arrogant people and humble people. A humble person realizes he is a sinner before God. He also glorifies God in all things, not himself. An arrogant man thinks only of himself and glorifies himself and not the Lord. Read the following scriptures and decide which category the person mentioned belongs to. (Answers are provided in the Answer Key.) Exodus 3:11; Exodus 5:2; I Samuel 18:18; Acts 20:16-19; Daniel 4:28-30; Joshua 7:6; Matthew 11:29; Daniel 4:37; II Chronicles 26:14-16; Esther 3:5.

"Food For Thought": Puzzles

- Who Said It? - Read each quotation listed below and decide who said it. Write the correct answer on the line. Answers are provided in the Answer Key. (All quotations are taken from the NKJV.)

1. "I fast twice a week." _____

2. "This man went down to his house justified rather than the other." _____

3. "God be merciful to me a sinner!" _____

4. "Two men went up to the temple to pray." _____

5. "I give tithes of all that I possess." _____

6. "He who humbles himself will be exalted." _____

7. "God, I thank You that I am not like other men." _____

8. "Everyone who exalts himself will be abased." _____

9. "The tax collector, standing afar off, would not so much as raise his eyes to heaven." _____

10. "The Pharisee stood and prayed thus with himself..." _____

- Who Prayed It? - There are several beautiful, heartfelt prayers recorded in the Bible. Look up each passage listed below and read the prayer. Then choose the name of who prayed it from the box and write it on the line. Answers are provided in the Answer Key.

Nehemiah	David	Hannah	Jabez	King Jehoshaphat	Jacob
	Moses	King Hezekiah	Jesus	Solomon	

1. I Chronicles 4:10 - _____

2. Nehemiah 1:5-11 - _____

3. II Chronicles 20:5-12 - _____

4. Psalm 51 - _____

5. II Kings 19:15-19 - _____

6. Luke 22:41-42 - _____

7. I Samuel 2:1-10 - _____

8. Exodus 33:12-13 - _____

9. I Kings 3:6-9 - _____

10. Genesis 32:9-12 - _____

"Fruits Of Our Labor": Crafts

- Humble/Proud Seesaw – Those who are humble lower themselves, but God lifts them up while those who are proud raise themselves, but God will lower them. Illustrate this with a seesaw craft. There are many different kinds of seesaws you can build from very simple tabletop models to full-size models in your backyard! Library books or online instructions (with permission) provide lots of cool ideas. However, a very simple way to make one is to use a toilet paper roll and a wide rectangular strip of cardboard which is securely taped or glued onto the roll. You could write the words "tax collector" on one end and "Pharisee" on the other, or make little figures to glue one on each end. Use your seesaw to tell someone the parable of the tax collector and the Pharisee. Demonstrate the attitude of the Pharisee and what happened to him as he went home versus the attitude of the tax collector and what happened to him as he went home.

- Illustrate a parable - Illustrate the parable from this lesson. You can continue the same method you have been using or choose a different way to illustrate it.

Lesson 13: Parable of the Rich Fool

Text: Luke 12:13-21

"Growing In The Word": Lesson Text & Discussion

Read Luke 12:13-14. In the beginning of this chapter, a huge crowd had gathered to hear Jesus, and he begins to teach them. When he finishes talking about the subject of hypocrisy and there is a pause, one man in the crowd pipes up with something that is on his mind. What does he want Jesus to do? (He wants Jesus to tell his brother to divide up the family inheritance.) Do you know what an inheritance is? To inherit something is to receive something such as money or property from someone who has died. The Jews had very specific inheritance laws as to how family property and possessions were to be divided among the children. (You will learn more about this in one of this lesson's research projects.) Evidently, this man did not feel like he was getting his "fair share." He wanted more, and he wanted Jesus to step in and help him get it. Was Jesus eager to help him? (No) Jesus doesn't want this young man (or any of us) to be focused on money and things and how we can get more, more, more! That is not what is important or of lasting value. Jesus wants us to focus on the things that are important to him, the things that truly matter. He is going to teach this young man and the crowd a parable about the dangers of covetousness.

Read Luke 12:15. Before beginning the parable, Jesus says, *"Beware of covetousness."* What does it mean to covet something? It is a very strong desire to have something. It is greediness. The young man who asked Jesus to step in to his family's inheritance dispute wasn't interested in Jesus righting a wrong; he was simply greedy to have more. **Read Exodus 20:17.** In the ten commandments, the last one warned against covetousness. God listed several things that His people were not to covet. What were they? (They were not to covet their neighbor's house, their neighbor's wife, their neighbor's servants, their neighbor's animals, or anything at all that belonged to their neighbor.) In other words, don't look at what someone else has and crave and desire to have it for yourself. What would be the opposite of always wanting what others have, of being covetous? (The opposite of covetousness is contentment.) To be content is to be happy and thankful for what you already have. After warning against covetousness, Jesus told the young man that life isn't about how much you have in possessions. Now he will illustrate that by talking about a rich farmer who kept wanting more.

Read Luke 12:16-18. What "problem" did the rich man have? (He didn't have room to store all of his crops.) That is a good problem to have! If you were a farmer, wouldn't you rather have too many crops to harvest and store than not enough? This rich farmer had been blessed with a very bountiful harvest, and that was a good thing. He realized that the barns he already had were not going to hold all of the harvest, and he wasn't about to let all of that extra food go to waste! So, what was his solution? (His solution was to tear down the barns he already had and build bigger barns to hold it all.) This may not sound all that bad. In fact, his solution might even seem wise. He had worked to plant a good crop and had been blessed with a particularly abundant harvest. He wasn't going to be wasteful or careless of the extra food, he was going to make provisions to store it all. So, what's the problem? Let's keep reading and find out.

Read Luke 12:19. Do you see a problem now? (Answers will vary.) His solution to store it all was so that he could keep it all for himself for years to come. He didn't consider that he might have been blessed so he could share with others who were in need. He didn't think to thank God for the bountiful harvest and then show generosity in giving back to Him. He only thought of himself and his own pleasures and comfort. **Read I Timothy 6:17-18.** God had a much better solution for the rich farmer than he had for himself. What do these verses command the rich to do? (The rich are to put their trust in the Lord, not in their riches. They are to do good, be ready to give and willing to share.) The rich farmer wasn't trusting in God to provide for his needs by blessing him with more good crops in the coming years, but instead, he was trusting in himself and what he already had and wanted to greedily hoard it up. How sad! If only he had applied the teaching in **Proverbs 3:9-10.** What does verse 9 say we should do with our possessions? (We should honor the Lord with them.) If we are generous in our giving to the Lord, if we are willing to do good and share with others, then we never have to worry if our "barns will be full." God will always provide us with everything we need. Not only that, he will give us *more* than we ever need. How does verse 10 describe the amount God will bless us with? (The barns would be filled with plenty and the vats would overflow with new wine.) When we honor the Lord with our possessions by giving to Him first, we will always be blessed. The rich farmer could have given away and shared so much of his bountiful harvest, and God would have just blessed him and replenished his supplies. The farmer never would have run out. God loves a cheerful giver (II Corinthians 9:7) and does not look kindly on a selfish, covetous heart.

Read Luke 12:20. What was God's response to the rich farmer's solution to all of his wealth? (He called him a fool and told him that he wouldn't live to enjoy all of those possessions he was hoarding up.) What is the opposite of foolishness? (Wisdom) This rich farmer was not wise at all in his decision about what to do with his riches. God says this man was foolish because he thought he had it all figured out: he would live for many years and sit back and enjoy all the things he had provided for himself, but God had a much different plan. What was going to happen to the rich farmer that very night? (He was going to die.) God told him, *"This night your soul will be required of you."* The farmer wasn't going to live another day, much less for years and years. What question did God ask him concerning all his possessions? ("*Whose will these things be which you have provided?*") The rich farmer was certainly not going to be around to enjoy his riches, so now, others would have them and receive the benefit of them.

Read Luke 12:21. Remember Jesus' warning before he began teaching this parable? "*Beware of covetousness.*" He ends this parable by saying that those who want to foolishly hoard up treasure for themselves and not be rich toward God are going to have a rude awakening like the rich farmer. Sometimes, it is easy for us to look at verses about the rich and the warnings given to them and think, "Yeah! Those rich people need to be nice and share!" But, let's think carefully about who exactly is rich...Many people in other countries live in shelters that we would barely call a home. I have visited the countries of Honduras, Haiti, and Jamaica and seen people living in cardboard shelters or pieces of tin and metal put together for them to sleep under. Many of these people in other countries don't have electricity, running water or an indoor toilet. Carpet, a mattress to sleep on, a kitchen with a full refrigerator? These are things most people in the world can only dream of. Do you have a solid roof over your head? Do you have electricity, running water, a flush toilet, food in your kitchen, clothes in your bedroom and more than one pair of shoes to wear? Then you are richer than about 80% of people in the world. God blesses us with so much. Let's work to have hearts that want to be rich toward Him.

Review Questions: (Answers are provided in the Answer Key.)

1. What did a man in the crowd tell Jesus to do?

2. How did Jesus respond to him?

3. Which of the ten commandments warned against covetousness?

4. What did God command His people not to covet in that commandment?

5. What is the opposite of covetousness?

6. In the beginning of the parable, what was the rich farmer's "problem"?

7. What was his solution to the problem?

8. According to I Timothy 6:17-18, what is the Lord's solution to the problem?

9. What does Proverbs 3:9-10 teach us to do with our possessions?

10. What did God say to the rich farmer?

11. Take a few moments to think about all of the things God has blessed you and your family with. Make a list if you'd like. After thinking it over for awhile, answer this question: Are you rich?

"Putting Down Roots": Memory Work

- Memorize Luke 12:15

- Matthew 6:20

- Matthew 6:21

- Hebrews 13:16

"Add A Leaf": Words To Know

- Covetousness

- Contentment

- Fool

"Harvest Fun": Games & Activities

- Gathering Grain – The rich farmer in this parable had a lot of grain to harvest! For this game, players will compete to find (harvest) the most grain in the time allotted. Use the template in Appendix B, printing out as many sheets as needed.

You may want to print them out on card stock and/or laminate them before cutting them apart. Let a scorekeeper hide the grain cards all over a large room or a house. When "Go" is called, let each player race to harvest as much grain as he can before time is up. After playing the game, discuss the parable. Was it wrong for the farmer to harvest so much grain? What *was* the problem?

- Get rid of your possessions! - This game is to be played like hot potato or the opposite of musical chairs. The goal is to *not* be caught holding onto something. Gather a couple of items to pass around such as a CD, a stuffed animal, a wallet, etc. (The number of items gathered will depend on the number of players. If only two or three are playing, use one item.) Players will sit in a circle with one or two players beginning the game with an item in their hand. Someone will start some music and players will begin to pass the items around the circle in a clockwise motion. When the music stops, whoever is holding onto a "possession" is out while the empty-handed players are still in. Let play continue until only one player is left. After playing, discuss the topic of covetousness. It is not wrong to have possessions, but our attitude toward them can be wrong if we are not careful. We want to make sure we are always willing to have a generous heart toward others.

"Digging Deeper": Research

- Covetousness word study – Use a concordance to help you learn more about the topic of covetousness. What was the Hebrew word for *covetousness* and what did it mean? What was the Greek word for *covetousness* and what did it mean? What Old Testament book contains at least four verses condemning or exposing the Israelites' sin of covetousness? Which Old Testament verse tells us "*he who hates covetousness will prolong his days*"? What New Testament scripture encourages "*let your conduct be without covetousness*"?

- Jewish Inheritance Laws – Jesus told this parable in response to a man who was not happy with the amount of inheritance he had received. Find out what you can about the Jewish laws concerning inheritance. How much did a firstborn son receive? If there were no sons, who would receive the inheritance? Was land able to pass from tribe to tribe? Read the following scriptures to help you answer these questions and check other resources such as a Bible dictionary as well. Numbers 27:8-11; Numbers 36:5-9; Deuteronomy 21:15-17.

"Food For Thought": Puzzles

- Word Scramble w/clues – Read the clues and unscramble the letters to form the answer. Answers are provided in the Answer Key.

1. v e t s c o n s e s u o – Jesus said to beware of this. _____

2. s e a t r u e r - We should not lay this up for ourselves. _____

3. s a n r b – Bigger ones were going to be built. _____

4. t h e n i n a r i c e – A man wanted his brother to divide this with him. _____

_____

5. d o u r n g – This yielded plentifully for the rich man. _____

6. l o f o – This is what God called the rich man. _____

7. s o p r c – This is what was going to be stored in the barns. _____

8. g i t s n h – Jesus said our lives do not consist in the abundance of this.

_____

9. u s l o – This was required of the rich man. _____

10. a b a r p l e – Jesus spoke this to the crowd. _____

- Parables Review – Match the clue on the left to the correct parable on the right. Answers are provided in the Answer Key.

_____ 1. This parable teaches persistence in prayer.

_____ 2. A woman searched her house diligently.

_____ 3. A man was beaten and left for dead.

_____ 4. Two kinds of animals were divided.

_____ 5. Beware of covetousness!

_____ 6. Show hospitality to those who can't repay.

_____ 7. A Jewish man had to feed pigs.

_____ 8. One showed no mercy to a fellow servant.

_____ 9. Ten, five, and one

_____ 10. A man sold all for something valuable.

_____ 11. Something tiny became something great.

_____ 12. A farmer sowed seed.

_____ 13. A man woke his friend in the middle of the night.

_____ 14. Men were hired throughout the day.

_____ 15. This parable teaches humility in prayer.

a. Parable of the Soils

b. Parable of the Talents

c. Parable of the Laborers

d. Parable of the Pharisee & Tax Collector

e. Parable of the Unforgiving Servant

f. Parable of the Mustard Seed

g. Parable of the Persistent Friend

h. Parable of the Rich Fool

i. Parable of the Lost Coin

j. Parable of the Pearl of Great Price

k. Parable of the Ambitious Guest

l. Parable of the Persistent Widow

m. Parable of the Lost Son

n. Parable of the Good Samaritan

o. Parable of the Sheep & Goats

"Fruits Of Our Labor": Crafts

- Wheat Weave – This is a weaving craft using ribbon to make puffy grains of wheat. You will need heavy card stock, a hole-puncher, ¾ inch or 1 inch wide light brown or tan ribbon and some tape. First, cut a rectangular piece of card stock 8 inches long by 3 inches wide. In the center of the rectangle, draw a thick brown or black line about 6 inches long, starting 1 ½ inches from the top. Next, draw an oval-shaped head of grain on the top of the line about an inch long, with points at each end. Then, draw identical heads of grain along the left and right sides of the line, six on one side and seven on the other, staggering them so they don't match up perfectly. Next, punch a hole near the top and base of each grain. Now, cut a 24-inch length of brown ribbon to do the threading. You will need to put a piece of tape around one end to create a threading end. It will look like the end of a shoelace. Now, you're ready to begin! Bring your ribbon up through one of the holes at the bottom of the card from the underside, leaving about ½ inch tail on the back. Turn the card over and tape the tail down securely. Now, poke the ribbon back down through the hole at the top of the grain head you began with. Keep threading all the way up one side, around the top, and back down the other side until you have threaded all of the heads of grain. Finish with threading the ribbon through at the back of the card, trimming it, and securing the tail with tape. If you'd like, write the words "Beware of covetousness" or "One's life does not consist in the abundance of things he possesses" from Luke 12:15 at the bottom of the card to remind you of the lesson from this parable.

- Illustrate the parable - Illustrate the parable from this lesson. You can continue the same method you have been using or choose a different way to illustrate it.

- Illustrated parables book – If you have been making illustrations of parables each lesson, it would really be nice to put them all together in a book. There's a couple of ways you can do this. First, you could design a front and back cover on card stock then laminate them for protection. Hole punch the covers and pages of your book and tie with ribbon to hold it together. If you want a little more professional book, you could purchase a bookbinding tool from bindingbooksbeautifully.com which allows you to drive nails through the layers at even intervals, remove the nails, then stitch your book together with thread. (Full instructions are included with the tool.)

Answer

Key

Answer Key

Lesson 1:

Review Questions:

1. What is the purpose of a parable? (The purpose of a parable is to teach a spiritual lesson.)

2. What is an example of a parable found in the Old Testament? (The story which Nathan the prophet told to King David in II Samuel 12 is an Old Testament example of a parable.)

3. What parable did Jesus teach in the beginning of Matthew 13? (The parable of the soils)

4. When we see the word "mystery" in the Bible, what does it mean? (It means something that is hidden, secret, or not yet revealed.)

5. Why did some people understand the parables of Jesus while others did not? (It depended on their hearts. Some people had hearts that were open to what Jesus was teaching them, while others had hard hearts that did not want to listen to or believe anything Jesus said to them.)

6. In what city did the church of Jesus Christ begin? (Jerusalem)

7. Where in the Bible do we read about the beginning of the church? (Acts 2)

8. What is inside a seed? (Life!)

9. How does the church grow? (The church grows when the seed, the Word of God, is planted in the hearts of people who are willing to love and obey the Lord.)

10. How is the kingdom of heaven like leaven? (It spreads and has influence wherever it goes and grows.)

11. What verse in the Old Testament prophesied that Jesus would open his mouth in parables? (Psalm 78:2)

12. How is the kingdom of heaven like hidden treasure? (It is more valuable than anything else, it is worth searching for, and it is worth sacrificing everything else in your life.)

13. In the parable of the pearl of great price, what is the kingdom of heaven compared to? (A merchant seeking beautiful pearls)

14. What are two differences in the parables of the hidden treasure and the pearl of great price? (1-The man who found the treasure found it by accident while the pearl merchant was deliberately looking for a valuable pearl. 2-The kingdom of heaven was compared to the valuable hidden treasure in the first parable while it was compared to the man and not the valuable pearl in the second parable.)

15. What does Matthew 6:33 tell us to seek? (The kingdom of God)

- Which Parable? - 1) Parable of the leaven, 2) Parable of the hidden treasure and Parable of the pearl of great price, 3) Parable of the mustard seed, 4) All four parables, 5) Parable of the hidden treasure, 6) Parable of the mustard seed and Parable of the hidden treasure, 7) Parable of the leaven and Parable of the hidden treasure, 8) Parable of the pearl of great price, 9) Parable of the hidden treasure and Parable of the pearl of great price, 10) Parable of the mustard seed

- Word Search Puzzle -

Lesson 2:

Review Questions:

1. Who stood up and asked Jesus a question? (A lawyer)

2. Why did he do this? (To test Jesus)

3. What question did he ask Jesus first? ("What shall I do to inherit eternal life?")

4. How did Jesus respond? (What does the law say?)

5. What two scriptures did the lawyer quote? (Deuteronomy 6:5 and Leviticus 19:18)

6. Did Jesus say the lawyer had answered right or wrong? (Right)

7. What was the next question the lawyer asked Jesus? ("Who is my neighbor?")

8. In the parable where was the traveler going? (Jericho)

9. What did the thieves do to the traveler? (Stripped him, wounded him, left him for dead)

10. Who passed by first? (A priest)

11. Who passed by second? (A Levite)

12. Who passed by third? (The Samaritan)

13. Who had compassion on the wounded man? (The Samaritan)

14. What did he do for the traveler? (Poured oil and wine on his wounds and bandaged them, took him to an inn and cared for him)

15. Whom did he pay to continue the man's care? (The innkeeper)

16. What did Jesus ask the lawyer at the conclusion of the parable? ("Which of these three do you think was neighbor to him who fell among the thieves?")

17. What answer did the lawyer give? ("He who showed mercy on him.")

18. What did Jesus tell him to do? (The same)

- Sequence -

__4__ A priest came down that road and passed by on the other side.

__2__ The lawyer, wanting to justify himself, asked Jesus, "Who is my neighbor?"

__8__ He took out two denarii and gave them to the innkeeper.

__3__ A man went down to Jericho and fell among thieves who left him half dead.

__9__ "Which of these three do you think was neighbor to him who fell among the thieves?"

__1__ A certain lawyer stood up and tested Jesus.

__5__ A Levite arrived at the place and looked, then passed by on the other side.

__7__ He went to him, bandaged his wounds, pouring on oil and wine.

__10__ Jesus said, "Go and do likewise".

__6__ A certain Samaritan saw him and had compassion on him.

Lesson 3:

Review Questions:

1. Who was Jesus eating with that wanted to hear him teach? (Tax collectors and sinners)

2. Who was murmuring about this? (Pharisees and scribes)

3. In the first parable, what was lost? (One sheep)

4. How many others were there who were in the wilderness? (Ninety-nine)

5. How did the man carry the lost one home? (On his shoulders)

6. When he arrived home, he called his friends and neighbors in to do what with him? (Rejoice)

7. Jesus said there is more joy in heaven over one sinner who does what? (Repents)

8. What did the woman lose in the second parable? (A silver coin)

9. How many other ones did she have? (Nine)

10. Where did she lose it? (In her house)

11. What did she do when she found it? (Rejoiced)

12. Who was lost in the third parable? (The younger son)

13. What did he ask his father for? (His inheritance)

14. What did he do with it? (Spent it all, wasted it)

15. What occurred in the land where he was living? (A famine)

16. What job did he get? (Feeding swine)

17. How hungry was he? (He wanted to eat the pigs' food.)

18. What is repentance? (Being sorry for sin which leads to a changed life)

19. What did he want to return home as? (A hired servant)

20. What did his father have the servants put on his son when he returned home? (The best robe, a ring on his hand, sandals on his feet)

21. What was killed for a feast of celebration? (Fatted calf)

22. What was the older son's reaction? (He was angry)

23. Who did Jesus come to seek and save? (The lost)

- Coded Message - "Repentance is being sorry for sin and turning to God."

- Crossword Puzzle – (Next page)

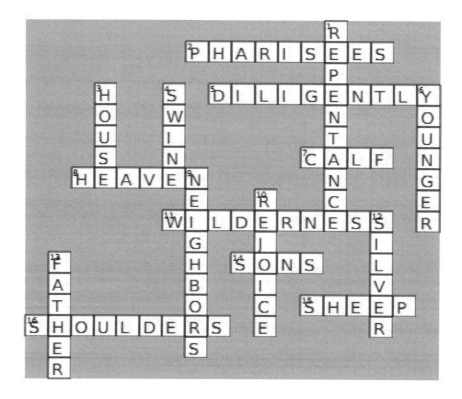

- The lost coin is in the pocket of the woman's dress in her bedroom closet.

Lesson 4:

Review Questions:

1. Up to how many times was Peter willing to forgive others? (Up to seven times)

2. How many times did Jesus say Peter should be willing to forgive? (Up to seventy times seven)

3. What did Jesus mean by that number? (It was not a literal number of how many times to forgive, but Jesus was teaching Peter to always forgive.)

4. How much did the servant who could not pay owe the king? (10,000 talents)

5. What did the king originally propose to help settle the debt? (The king ordered that the servant, his wife, his children and all his possessions be sold.)

6. How did the servant respond to the king's original command? (He fell down before the king and begged for patience and time to pay.)

7. What did the servant promise the king that he would never be able to do? (He promised to pay all of the debt.)

8. When the king was moved with compassion, what did he do to help the servant? (He forgave the debt he owed.)

9. What was the first thing the servant did after being released by the king? (He found someone who owed him money and demanded repayment.)

10. What was interesting about what the fellow servant did and said? (It was exactly the same as what the unforgiving servant did and said to the king.)

11. What was done to the fellow servant who could not pay his debt? (He was thrown into prison until he could pay.)

12. Who told the king what the unforgiving servant had done? (His fellow servants)

13. How did the king refer to the unforgiving servant? (He called him a wicked servant.)

14. What punishment was ordered by the king? (The unforgiving servant was to be turned over to the torturers until the debt was paid in full.)

15. Will God forgive us if we are unwilling to forgive others? (No)

- True or False – 1) True, 2) False, 3) False, 4) True, 5) False, 6) True, 7) True, 8) False, 9) True, 10) False

- Matching – 1) D, 2) G, 3) H, 4) J, 5) B, 6) I, 7) F, 8) A, 9) E, 10) C

Lesson 5:

Review Questions:

1. In the parable of the talents, how many servants did the man have and what did he give to each one of them before traveling on his journey? (He had three

servants. To one he gave five talents, to another he gave two talents and to the third one he gave one talent.)

2. How did the master decide how much to trust each servant with? (He divided the talents among them according to their abilities.)

3. How many of the servants increased their share of their master's money? (Two of the servants made a profit with their share.)

4. What did the one-talent servant do with his share of his master's money? (He buried it in the ground.)

5. How did the master refer to the five and two-talent servants? (He called them good and faithful.)

6. What two rewards does the master give to these servants? (1-He tells the servants he will make them ruler over many things because they were faithful over a few. 2-They're also invited to enter into the joy of their lord.)

7. How did the one-talent man refer to his master? (He called him a hard man.)

8. Was this true about the master? (No)

9. What did the master call the one-talent man? (He called him wicked and lazy.)

10. What does Proverbs 12:24 tell us that the hand of the diligent will do? (It will rule.)

11. What was the easiest thing the one-talent man should have at least done with the master's money? (He should have put it in the bank to earn interest.)

12. What did the master order to be done with the one-talent man's talent? (He ordered it to be taken away from him.)

13. Who was it given to? (It was given to the man with ten talents.)

14. What was the one-talent man's punishment? (He was cast into outer darkness.)

15. How does the master refer to this servant as his punishment is announced? (He calls him an unprofitable servant.)

- What's Missing?

1. "And I was __afraid__ , and went and __hid__ your __talent__ in the __ground__ . Look, there you have what is __yours__ ." (Matthew 25:25)

2. "And to one he gave __five__ talents, to another __two__ , and to another __one__ , to each according to his own __ability__ ; and immediately he went on a __journey__ ." (Matthew 25:15)

3. "For to __everyone__ who has, __more__ will be given, and he will have __abundance__ ; but from him who does not __have__ , even what he __has__ will be __taken__ __away__ ." (Matthew 25:29)

4. "So he who had received __five__ talents came and brought __five__ other talents, saying, 'Lord, you delivered to me __five__ talents; look, I have gained __five__ more talents beside them.'" (Matthew 25:20)

5. "His __lord__ said to him, 'Well done, good and __faithful__ servant; you have been __faithful__ over a __few__ things, I will make you __ruler__ over __many__ things. Enter into the __joy__ of your __lord__ .'" (Matthew 25:23)

Lesson 6:

Review Questions:

1. What was Jesus teaching his disciples about in the first four verses of Luke 11? (Prayer)

2. What time of night was the scene of the parable set? (Midnight)

3. What was the problem in this parable? (A visitor had arrived at someone's house and their was no food to offer him.)

4. How many loaves of bread did the man ask to borrow from his friend? (Three)

5. Why did the friend say "No" at first? (He said his door was shut, or locked, and everyone in the house was in bed asleep so he did not want to be troubled to get up and answer the door.)

6. Why was the man successful in borrowing bread from his friend? (He was persistent.)

7. What are three ways God answers our prayers? (Yes, no, wait)

8. According to Jesus, how often should we pray? (Always)

9. Who were the two main characters in the second parable? (A judge and a widow)

10. Describe the judge. (He was a man who did not fear God or care about other people.)

11. What did the widow want the judge to do for her? (She wanted him to avenge her of her adversary.)

12. Was the judge moved with pity by the widow's case? (No)

13. What made the judge finally decide to rule in her favor? (The persistence of the widow)

14. Is God like the judge in this parable? (No)

15. How does God avenge His own people? (Speedily)

16. What does Jesus want to find on the earth when he comes again one day? (Faith)

17. Will you be faithful to God?

- Who Said It? - 1) Jesus, 2) The persistent friend, 3) The friend within, 4) The widow, 5) The Lord, 6) The unjust judge, 7) Jesus, 8) The persistent friend, 9) The friend within, 10) Jesus

- Word Scramble – 1) persistent, 2) judge, 3) adversary, 4) prayer, 5) widow, 6) avenge, 7) neighbor, 8) parables, 9) midnight, 10) loaves

Lesson 7:

Review Questions:

1. What size crowd did Jesus teach this parable to? (A great multitude)

2. How would a sower sow his seed in ancient times? (He took handfuls of seed and scattered it over the ground.)

3. What does it mean "to sow"? (It means to scatter seed.)

4. What were the four kinds of soil Jesus mentioned in this parable? (1-The wayside, 2-Rocky, 3-Thorny ground, 4-Good soil)

5. Which one of our five physical senses (seeing, hearing, smelling, tasting, touching) was Jesus emphasizing? (Hearing)

6. What did the seed represent in this parable? (The Word of God)

7. Who snatches the soil out of the wayside heart? (Satan)

8. What is the problem with the hearts that are like the rocky soil? (They have no root. They are shallow, being easily distracted by the temptations of the world.)

9. What are three things Jesus says the thorns represent? (1-Cares, 2-Riches, 3-Pleasures of life)

10. How does Jesus describe the heart that is like the good ground? (Noble and good)

11. How does one bear fruit for the Lord? (Answers will vary but may include things such as serving others, teaching the gospel, practicing the fruits of the Spirit listed in Galatians 5:22-23.)

12. What kind of soil is your heart?

- Coded Message - "But the ones that fell on the good ground are those who having heard the word with a noble and good heart keep it and bear fruit with patience." Luke 8:15

- Sequence – 1) **8**, 2) **3**, 3) **6**, 4) **5**, 5) **1**, 6) **10**, 7) **4**, 8) **9**, 9) **2**, 10) **7**

Lesson 8:

Review Questions:

1. How many sons did the man in the parable have? (Two)

2. What did the father command his sons to do? (He told them to go and work in his vineyard.)

3. When did the work need to be done. (That very day)

4. How would you describe the way the first son answered his father? (Rudely, disrespectfully, etc.)

5. How did the first son respond to his father's request? (He said he wouldn't go work, but later he regretted that and went to work in the vineyard.)

6. List some examples from the Bible of people who refused to obey God for awhile but then later changed their mind and obeyed Him. (Answers will vary.)

7. What is repentance? (Repentance is being sorry for sin, but then changing your life.)

8. How did the second son respond to his father's request? (He said he would go work, but he didn't go.)

9. What verse in the New Testament tells us that those who do the will of the Father will enter the kingdom of heaven? (Matthew 7:21)

10. In this parable, which son did the will of his father? (The first one)

11. To whom was Jesus teaching this parable? (The chief priests and elders of the people)

12. To which son in the parable did Jesus compare them to? (The second son)

13. Who did the father in the parable represent? (God)

14. Why would tax collectors and harlots enter the kingdom of heaven before the people Jesus was talking to? (The tax collectors and harlots were unbelievers and

sinners who came to repentance and obeyed the Lord, doing His will while the religious leaders of the Jews appeared to be religious but didn't do God's will.)

15. Who had come to the Jews preaching righteous but was not believed? (John the baptist)

16. What two groups of people did believe the preaching? (Tax collectors and harlots)

- What's Missing? -

1. "For __John__ came to __you__ in the way of __righteousness__, and you did not __believe__ him." (Matthew 21:32)

2. "Which of the __two__ did the __will__ of his __father__?" (Matthew 21:31)

3. "A man had two __sons__, and he came to the __first__ and said, '__Son__, go, __work__ today in my __vineyard__.'" (Matthew 21:28)

4. "Then he came to the __second__ and said __likewise__. And he __answered__ and said, 'I go, __sir__,' but he did not __go__." (Matthew 21:30)

5. "He __answered__ and said, 'I will __not__,' but __afterward__ he __regretted__ it and __went__." (Matthew 21:29)

- To obey or not to obey? -

1. Genesis 6:22 – Who obeyed God? __Noah__ How much of what God commanded him did he obey? __He obeyed all that God commanded him.__

2. Haggai 1:7-8, 12 – Who obeyed God? __Zerubbabel, Joshua, and the people__

   What had God told them to do? __He had told them to rebuild the temple__

3. Leviticus 10:1 – Who disobeyed God? __Nadab and Abihu__

   How had they disobeyed Him? __They offered fire that God had not authorized them to use.__

4. John 8:29 – Who is speaking in this verse? __Jesus__ How often did he do things that pleased God? ___He always did things that would please his Father God.___

5. I Samuel 15:1-3, 7-9 – What command did God give in verses 1-3? _God commanded King Saul to completely destroy the Amalekites, both people and animals. Nothing was to be spared._

   Was that command obeyed? __No__ Why or why not? _Saul thought that obeying part of what God said was good enough, but it wasn't. Even though he thought he had a good reason for sparing some of the animals, God did not accept that and was not at all pleased because Saul did not obey what he was commanded to do._

Lesson 9:

Review Questions:

1. According to the law of Moses, when were day laborers to be paid? (At the end of the day's work)

2. Where did the landowner want work to be done? (In his vineyard)

3. When did the landowner hire the first group of workers? (In the morning)

4. How many times in all did the landowner hire a group of workers throughout the day? (5 times – the morning, the 3rd hour, the 6th hour, the 9th hour, and the 11th hour)

5. Who was in charge of paying the laborers? (The steward of the landowner)

6. What Old Testament steward was mentioned in this lesson? (Joseph)

7. In what order were the workers to be paid? (Those who were hired last were to be paid first down to those who were hired first were to be paid last.)

8. How much was paid to the workers who had been hired at the 11th hour? (A denarius)

9. How long had these men worked in the vineyard? (One hour)

10. When the men who had been hired first thing in the morning saw this, what did they think it meant for them? (They thought they would be paid more.)

11. What were these men paid? (A denarius)

12. Were these workers satisfied with such payment? (No)

13. What did they say to the landowner about their wages as compared to what the other men were paid? (They complained that it wasn't fair that they were all paid the same amount when some had only worked one hour and they had worked hard the entire day.)

14. Did the landowner pay them what he had agreed to pay them that morning? (Yes)

15. Was this landowner a generous man? (Yes)

16. What does Philippians 2:14 remind us to do? (It reminds us to do everything without murmuring or complaining.)

17. According to Jesus, who will be first and who will be last? (The last will be first, and the first will be last.)

18. Does the age you become a Christian and years of service you have in the kingdom of God determine how much of a reward you will receive from God? (No)

19. What is grace? (Grace is when we receive what we do not deserve.)

20. What is God's gift of grace to us? (Salvation)

- Research: Jewish Day – The Jewish day started at sunset or around 6:00 p.m. and was divided into 8 equal parts, four watches of the night and four watches of the day. The first watch of the day began at 6:00 a.m. which ended the fourth watch of the night. So, the first hour of the day would be 7:00 a.m. and the 12th or last hour of the day would be 6:00 p.m. Jesus said in John 11:9, *Are there not twelve hours in the day?* 3Rd hour - __9:00 a.m.__, 6th hour - __12:00 p.m. (noon)__, 9th hour - __3:00 p.m.__, 11th hour - __5:00 p.m.__

- True or False? - 1) True, 2) False, 3) False, 4) True, 5) False, 6) True, 7) True, 8) True, 9) False, 10) True

- What Happened Next? -

1. A landowner went out early in the morning to hire laborers to work in his vineyard. <u>He agreed with the laborers for a denarius a day, then sent them to work.</u>

2. The landowner went into the marketplace about the 3rd hour of the day and saw some standing idle. <u>He told them to go work in his vineyard, and he would pay them what was right.</u>

3. He went out about the 11th hour of the day and found others standing idle. <u>He asked them why they had been standing idle all day.</u>

4. The workers who were hired first in the morning received their wages. <u>They murmured against the landowner.</u>

5. The landowner told the workers who had been hired first that they had received the wages that had been agreed upon. <u>He told them to take what was theirs and go their way.</u>

Lesson 10:

Review Questions:

1. Who had invited people to dine at his house? (A Pharisee)

2. What did Jesus notice about the guests who had arrived? (They were seating themselves in the best places.)

3. If you were practicing good manners, where would you sit at a feast you were invited to? (You would seat yourself in a lowly place, not the best seat.)

4. When someone is humble, whose interests does he consider? (He thinks about others interests above his own.)

5. What does Jesus say will happen to those who exalt themselves? (They will be brought low.)

6. What does Jesus say will happen to those who humble themselves? (They will be exalted.)

7. Whom does Jesus tell the host not to invite to dinner? (The rich, his family, his friends)

8. Whom does Jesus tell the host he should invite to dinner? (The poor, crippled and blind – those who cannot repay such a kindness)

9. In the second parable, the Great Supper, what happened to the first set of guests who had been invited? (None of them came to the banquet; they all had excuses.)

10. What was the reaction of the master to all of this? (He was angry.)

11. What did the master command his servant to do? (He told him to go out into the streets and bring in the poor, crippled, and blind to the feast.)

12. Did this fill all of the seats at the banquet? (No)

13. What was the next command the master gave his servant? (He told him to go out again into the highways and bushes and bring in anyone he could find.)

14. Who would *not* be at the great banquet? (None of those who had originally been invited would be there.)

15. In the second parable, who does the master represent and what does the invitation to the banquet represent? (The master represents God who invites us to enter His kingdom.)

- Which parable? - 1) The Great Feast, 2) The Ambitious Guests, 3) Both, 4) The Ambitious Guests, 5) Both, 6) The Great Feast, 7) The Great Feast, 8) The Ambitious Guests or both, 9) The Ambitious Guests, 10) Both

- Search the Scriptures -

poor

1. "But when you give a feast, invite the ~~rich~~, the maimed, the lame, the blind." (Luke 14:13)

first

2. "But they all with one accord began to make excuses. The ~~third~~ one said to him, 'I

piece of ground   it

have bought a ~~yoke of oxen~~, and I must go and see ~~them~~. I ask you to have me

excused

~~another time~~." (Luke 14:18)

feast   best place

3. "When you are invited to a wedding ~~ceremony~~, do not sit down in the ~~front row~~,

honorable

lest one more ~~important~~ than you be invited by him." (Luke 14:8)

his servant   highways

4. "Then the master said to ~~the mistress~~, 'Go out into the ~~alleys~~ and hedges, and

compel   house

~~beg~~ them to come in, that my ~~castle~~ may be filled.'" (Luke 14:23)

parable   invited

5. "So He told a ~~story~~ to those who were ~~there~~, when He noted how they chose the

best

~~quietest~~ places." (Luke 14:7)

Lesson 11:

Review Questions:

1. Who is the "Son of Man?" (Jesus Christ)

2. On the day of judgment, where will he set the sheep and where will he set the goats? (The sheep will be placed at his right hand and the goats at his left hand.)

3. Which position was a place of favor and honor? (To be placed at the right hand was special.)

4. Who calls the sheep, *"you blessed of My Father"*? (The King)

5. What inheritance will the sheep receive? (The kingdom that was prepared for them.)

6. When was this inheritance prepared by God? (Before the world was ever created)

7. Why was the King pleased with the sheep? (He was pleased at all of their kind and compassionate acts of service they had done to Him.)

8. Why did the righteous question what the King praised them for? (They didn't think they had ever actually done any acts of service for the King himself. They had done simply done them for other people as they saw the needs and didn't feel deserving of such praise.)

9. How did the King answer them? (He told them that every time they had done something for someone else in need, it was the same as doing it to the King himself.)

10. According to Colossians 3:23-24, who are we ultimately serving as we go about serving others? (The Lord Jesus Christ)

11. What is the opposite of righteousness? (Wickedness)

12. Where were the goats to be sent as punishment? (They were to be sent into everlasting fire.)

13. Who else would be there? (The devil and his angels)

14. What excuse did the wicked offer for not serving the Lord? (They said they never saw Him in need.)

15. Was this excuse acceptable to the King? (No)

16. What does James 4:17 tell us about failing to do good when we know we should do it? (It is sin.)

17. Where does Jesus say the righteous will go? (They will go into eternal life.)

• Matching – 1) e, 2) f, 3) g, 4) i, 5) h, 6) b, 7) j, 8) c, 9) a, 10) d

• Crossword Puzzle -

Lesson 12:

Review Questions:

1. To whom did Jesus tell this parable? (He told it to those who thought of themselves as very righteous while looking down their noses and despising others.)

2. What chapter in Matthew is full of Jesus' condemnation of the Pharisees? (Matthew 23)

3. What was the Pharisees' problem? (They were hypocrites. They did not practice what they preached to the people.)

4. Where did the Pharisee and tax collector go to pray? (To the temple)

5. Describe the Pharisee's prayer. (Answers will vary but should include that it was boastful and proud, self-righteous.)

6. What four groups of people did the Pharisee mention in his prayer that he was thankful he was "not like"? (Extortioners, unjust, adulterers and tax collectors)

7. What good works did the Pharisee list in his prayer? (Fasting and tithing)

8. What was the tax collector doing as he prayed? (He looked down at the ground and beat on his chest.)

9. Quote the tax collector's prayer. ("God be merciful to me a sinner!")

10. Which prayer did Jesus say was acceptable? (The tax collector's prayer)

11. What happens to someone who lifts themselves up in pride? (They will be brought low.)

12. What happens to those who humble themselves? (They will be lifted up or exalted.)

13. What New Testament scripture tells us what will happen if we humble ourselves in the sight of the Lord? (James 4:10)

- Acceptable Prayer – Proverbs 28:19 - Unacceptable; I John 5:14 - Acceptable; Exodus 34:8-9 - Acceptable; Psalm 66:18 - Unacceptable; James 4:3 - Unacceptable; Philippians 4:6-7 - Acceptable; I Thessalonians 5:16-18 - Acceptable; James 1:6b-8 - Unacceptable; Matthew 6:7 - Unacceptable; Proverbs 21:13 – Unacceptable

- Humble/Arrogant - Exodus 3:11, Moses - Humble; Exodus 5:2, Pharaoh - Arrogant; I Samuel 18:18, David - Humble; Acts 20:16-19, Paul - Humble; Daniel 4:28-30, King Nebuchadnezzar - Arrogant; Joshua 7:6, Joshua & the elders of Israel - Humble; Matthew 11:29, Jesus - Humble; Daniel 4:37, King Nebuchadnezzar - Humble; II Chronicles 26:14-16, King Uzziah - Arrogant; Esther 3:5, Haman - Arrogant.

- Who Said It? - 1) Pharisee, 2) Jesus, 3) Tax Collector, 4) Jesus, 5) Pharisee, 6) Jesus, 7) Pharisee, 8) Jesus, 9) Jesus, 10) Jesus

- Who Prayed It? - 1) Jabez, 2) Nehemiah, 3) King Jehoshaphat, 4) David, 5) Hezekiah, 6) Jesus, 7) Hannah, 8) Moses, 9) Solomon, 10) Jacob

Lesson 13:

Review Questions:

1. What did a man in the crowd tell Jesus to do? (He told him to tell his brother to divide the family inheritance with him.)

2. How did Jesus respond to him? (He told him it wasn't his place to deal with such a matter.)

3. Which of the ten commandments warned against covetousness? (The 10th commandment)

4. What did God command His people not to covet in that commandment? (He commanded His people not to covet their neighbor's house, or his wife, or his servants, or his animals, or anything that belonged to him.)

5. What is the opposite of covetousness? (Contentment)

6. In the beginning of the parable, what was the rich farmer's "problem"? (He didn't have enough room to store all of his crops.)

7. What was his solution to the problem? (He was going to tear down the barns he already had and build bigger barns to hold all of the harvest.)

8. According to I Timothy 6:17-18, what is the Lord's solution to the problem? (The Lord wants those who are rich to trust in Him and not their riches, to do good, to give to others and to share.)

9. What does Proverbs 3:9-10 teach us to do with our possessions? (We are to honor the Lord with them.)

10. What did God say to the rich farmer? (He called him a fool and told him that his soul would be required that very night.)

- Word Scramble w/clues – 1) covetousness, 2) treasure, 3) barns, 4) inheritance, 5) ground, 6) fool, 7) crops, 8) things, 9) soul, 10) parable

- Parables Review – 1) l, 2) i, 3) n, 4) o, 5) h, 6) k, 7) m, 8) e, 9) b, 10) j, 11) f, 12) a, 13) g, 14) c, 15) d

Appendix B – Templates

Lesson 3 – Lost Coin Picture, 2 pages

Lesson 5 – Talent template

Lesson 6 – Loaf of Bread template

Lesson 13 – Grain templates

*Each item may be photocopied for personal home use as much as needed.

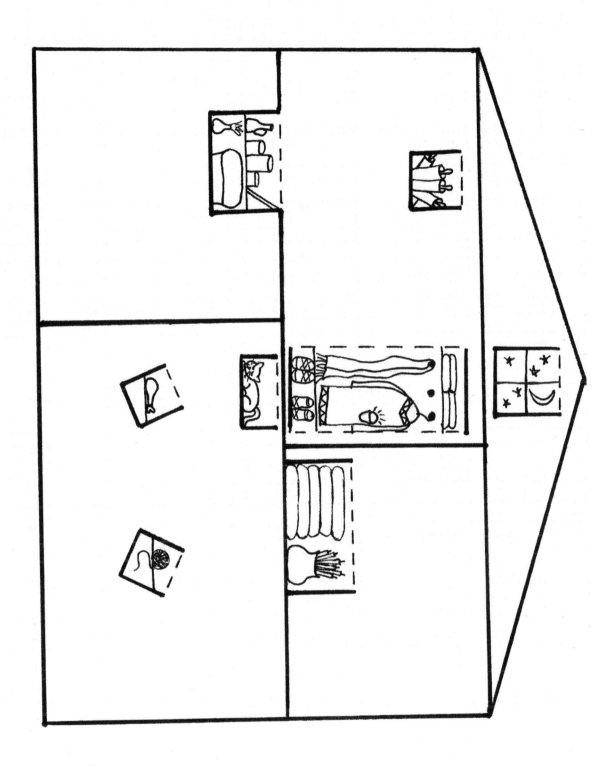

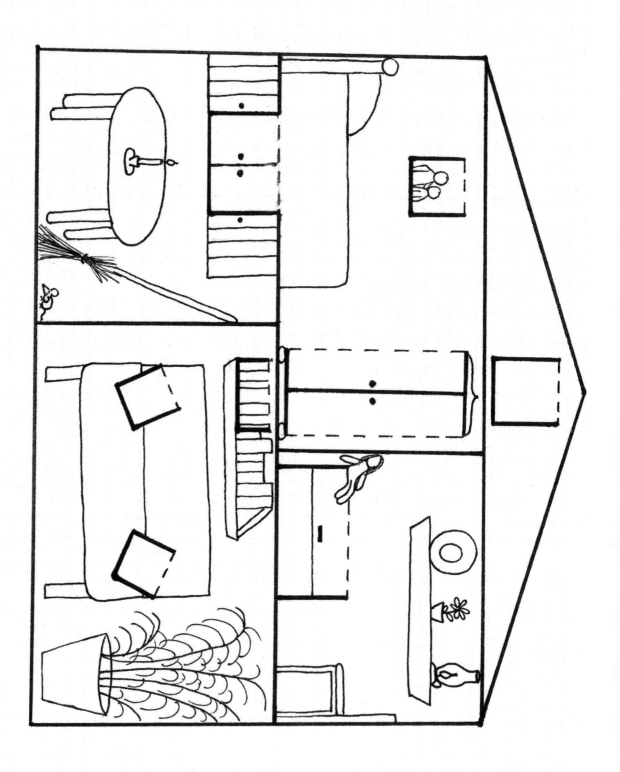

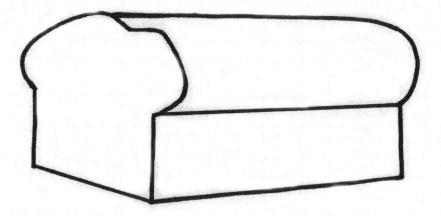

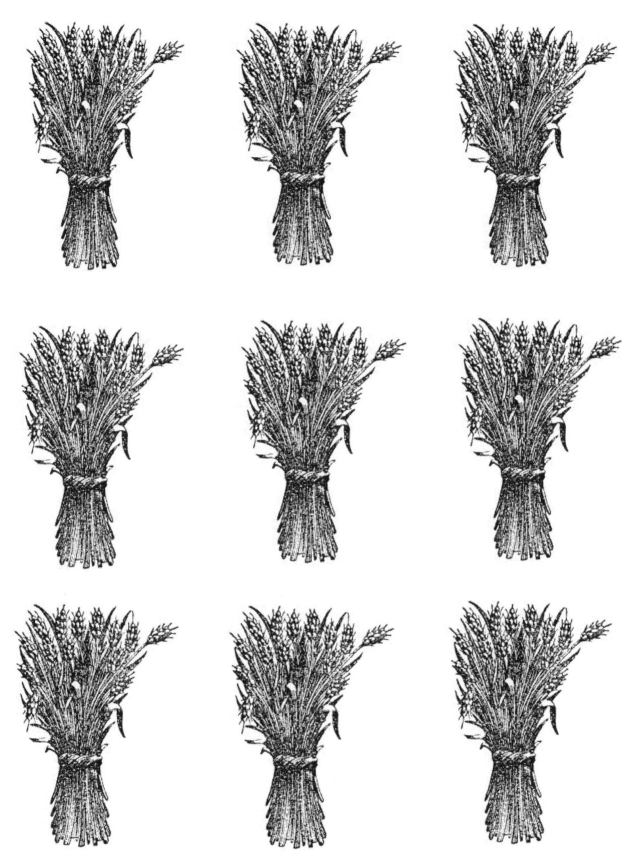

Made in the USA
Middletown, DE
27 September 2023

39391397R00084